Poems *to* Learn *by* Heart

By the same author:

The Book Lovers' Companion: What to Read Next (ed.)

I Wandered Lonely as a Cloud: … and other poems you half remember from school (ed.)

Tyger Tyger Burning Bright: Much-Loved Poems You Half Remember (ed.)

Poems *to* Learn *by* Heart

ANA SAMPSON

Michael O'Mara Books Ltd

First published in Great Britain in 2013 by
Michael O'Mara Books Limited
9 Lion Yard
Tremadoc Road
London SW4 7NQ

A CIP catalogue record for this book is available
from the British Library.

Papers used by Michael O'Mara Books Limited are natural,
recyclable products made from wood grown in sustainable forests.
The manufacturing processes conform to the environmental
regulations of the country of origin.

ISBN: 978-1-78243-145-9 in hardback print format

5 7 9 10 8 6 4

Designed and typeset by www.glensaville.com
Cover design/illustration by Patrick Knowles
Printed and bound by CPI Group (UK) Ltd, Croydon, CR0 4YY

www.mombooks.com

Contents

To Sophie, for when you're ready for words.

Introduction

Reading poetry – letting phrases wash over you and seizing on the passages that best describe a certain feeling – is a wonderful way to spend time. Committing those same poems to memory, so you have within yourself a storehouse of the most beautiful and, I would argue, useful words in the language, is hugely rewarding and a skill worth cultivating.

Some might argue that learning by rote is obsolete in our technological age in which we can, at any moment, reach out through cyberspace and grasp the words of a slightly remembered poem. But these no doubt enthusiastic sharers of poetry aren't always careful with their words, with many a variation of even the most well-known poems appearing online. If this isn't enough to deter you, knowing the poems by heart means they will become a part of your consciousness in a way that can never be replicated by calling them up on a smartphone screen.

In previous generations it was common to learn reams of verse and, today, there is an appetite to resurrect this practice. The process confers educational advantages – an enhanced vocabulary, improved retention of knowledge, familiarity with the canon – but there are other benefits, more lasting, more significant and more delightful, to learning poetry.

These advantages were summarized wonderfully by literary critic John Walsh, who likened learning poems by heart to 'having your own private internal iPoems library', adding, 'It's about owning someone else's words, but making them part of your life, your thoughts and your heart.'[1]

To store up a memory bank of poems is to build up your own unique library for life. The verses are your personal armoury against the slings and arrows of life – be they a lover's cruelty,

---

1   *The Independent*, January 2013

illness, or even just an irritatingly delayed train. Survivors of traumatic events, such as the hostage Terry Waite, recall reciting poetry learned by heart during their darkest hours, and when memory fades in the elderly, it is often the rhymes learned as children that are retained longest.

If you are new to learning poems by heart, I would recommend starting with shorter verses. Look, too, for poems with a strong rhyme scheme and a steady rhythm. Most importantly, choose a poem that you love, and that you would like to add to your mental furniture.

Once you've chosen a poem, write it out on a piece of paper to get a feel for the lines. Read it aloud several times, and you may find it helpful to walk in time with the poem's rhythm and recite the words in time with your footsteps. Take it line by line: recite the first line until it is perfect (choosing a very famous poem will help here, as you will likely already know the opening) then add the second, and so on. Do not learn a new line until you can recite the previous lines perfectly. You might find it helpful to recite the poem daily, and attaching visual cues (or other prompts) to each line of the poem will enable you to walk through the lines without forgetting what comes next. Before long, the poem is yours: caught fast in memory and ready to be recalled when wanted and needed.

This anthology is divided thematically to help you discover more easily the right poem for every occasion. I apologize for the no doubt countless omissions, and hope that this necessarily small selection will inspire you to seek out other verses with which to fill the shelves in your inner library. Most of all, I hope that you will discover and cherish the pleasures of learning and knowing poetry by heart.

Ana Sampson
London, 2013

One

Is there anybody there?: Magic

Poetry conjures up imaginary worlds of magic and mystery in a far more unfettered way than prose or the paintbrush. What better words to have stored in your memory than the incantations that transport us so easily from the humdrum daily world? Here is the escape hatch from the commute, the queue and the waiting room.

William Allingham (1824–89)

The Fairies

Up the airy mountain,
   Down the rushy glen,
We daren't go a-hunting
   For fear of little men;
Wee folk, good folk,
   Trooping all together;
Green jacket, red cap,
   And white owl's feather!

Down along the rocky shore
   Some make their home,
They live on crispy pancakes
   Of yellow tide-foam;
Some in the reeds
   Of the black mountain lake,
With frogs for their watch-dogs,
   All night awake.

High on the hill-top
   The old King sits;
He is now so old and gray
   He's nigh lost his wits.
With a bridge of white mist
   Columbkill he crosses,
On his stately journeys
   From Slieveleague to Rosses;
Or going up with music
   On cold starry nights
To sup with the Queen
   Of the gay Northern Lights.

They stole little Bridget
    For seven years long;
When she came down again
    Her friends were all gone.
They took her lightly back,
    Between the night and morrow,
They thought that she was fast asleep,
    But she was dead with sorrow.
They have kept her ever since
    Deep within the lake,
On a bed of flag-leaves,
    Watching till she wake.

By the craggy hill-side,
    Through the mosses bare,
They have planted thorn-trees
    For pleasure here and there.
Is any man so daring
    As dig them up in spite,
He shall find their sharpest thorns
    In his bed at night.

Up the airy mountain,
    Down the rushy glen,
We daren't go a-hunting
    For fear of little men;
Wee folk, good folk,
    Trooping all together;
Green jacket, red cap,
    And white owl's feather!

Samuel Taylor Coleridge (1772–1834)

Kubla Khan, or A Vision in a Dream. A Fragment.

This is a wonderful poem for those times when you would like to drift away (but when it would be imprudent to indulge in opium, as its author did).

In Xanadu did Kubla Khan
A stately pleasure-dome decree:
Where Alph, the sacred river, ran
Through caverns measureless to man
    Down to a sunless sea.
So twice five miles of fertile ground
With walls and towers were girdled round:
And there were gardens bright with sinuous rills,
Where blossomed many an incense-bearing tree;
And here were forests ancient as the hills,
Enfolding sunny spots of greenery.
But oh! that deep romantic chasm which slanted
Down the green hill athwart a cedarn cover!
A savage place! as holy and enchanted
As e'er beneath a waning moon was haunted
By woman wailing for her demon-lover!
And from this chasm, with ceaseless turmoil seething,
As if this earth in fast thick pants were breathing,
A mighty fountain momently was forced:
Amid whose swift half-intermitted burst
Huge fragments vaulted like rebounding hail,
Or chaffy grain beneath the thresher's flail:
And 'mid these dancing rocks at once and ever
It flung up momently the sacred river.
Five miles meandering with a mazy motion

Through wood and dale the sacred river ran,
Then reached the caverns measureless to man,
And sank in tumult to a lifeless ocean:
And 'mid this tumult Kubla heard from far
Ancestral voices prophesying war!
    The shadow of the dome of pleasure
    Floated midway on the waves;
    Where was heard the mingled measure
    From the fountain and the caves.
    It was a miracle of rare device,
    A sunny pleasure-dome with caves of ice!

    A damsel with a dulcimer
    In a vision once I saw:
    It was an Abyssinian maid,
    And on her dulcimer she played,
    Singing of Mount Abora.
    Could I revive within me
    Her symphony and song,
    To such a deep delight 'twould win me,
That with music loud and long,
I would build that dome in air,
That sunny dome! those caves of ice!
And all who heard should see them there,
And all should cry, Beware! Beware!
His flashing eyes, his floating hair!
Weave a circle round him thrice,
And close your eyes with holy dread,
For he on honey-dew hath fed,
And drunk the milk of Paradise.

W.B. Yeats (1865–1939)

The Song of the Wandering Aengus

I went out to the hazel wood,
Because a fire was in my head,
And cut and peeled a hazel wand,
And hooked a berry to a thread;
And when white moths were on the wing,
And moth-like stars were flickering out,
I dropped the berry in a stream
And caught a little silver trout.

When I had laid it on the floor
I went to blow the fire a-flame,
But something rustled on the floor,
And some one called me by my name:
It had become a glimmering girl
With apple blossom in her hair
Who called me by my name and ran
And faded through the brightening air.

Though I am old with wandering
Through hollow lands and hilly lands,
I will find out where she has gone,
And kiss her lips and take her hands;
And walk among long dappled grass,
And pluck till time and times are done,
The silver apples of the moon,
The golden apples of the sun.

Elizabeth Barrett Browning (1806–61)

A Musical Instrument

What was he doing, the great god Pan,
    Down in the reeds by the river?
Spreading ruin and scattering ban,
Splashing and paddling with hoofs of a goat,
And breaking the golden lilies afloat
    With the dragon-fly on the river.

He tore out a reed, the great god Pan,
    From the deep cool bed of the river;
The limpid water turbidly ran,
And the broken lilies a-dying lay,
And the dragon-fly had fled away,
    Ere he brought it out of the river.

High on the shore sat the great god Pan,
    While turbidly flow'd the river;
And hack'd and hew'd as a great god can
With his hard bleak steel at the patient reed,
Till there was not a sign of the leaf indeed
    To prove it fresh from the river.

He cut it short, did the great god Pan
    (How tall it stood in the river!),
Then drew the pith, like the heart of a man,
Steadily from the outside ring,
And notch'd the poor dry empty thing
    In holes, as he sat by the river.

'This is the way,' laugh'd the great god Pan
    (Laugh'd while he sat by the river),
'The only way, since gods began

To make sweet music, they could succeed.'
Then dropping his mouth to a hole in the reed,
    He blew in power by the river.

Sweet, sweet, sweet, O Pan!
    Piercing sweet by the river!
Blinding sweet, O great god Pan!
The sun on the hill forgot to die,
And the lilies revived, and the dragon-fly
    Came back to dream on the river.

Yet half a beast is the great god Pan,
    To laugh as he sits by the river,
Making a poet out of a man:
The true gods sigh for the cost and pain—
For the reed which grows nevermore again
    As a reed with the reeds of the river.

Alfred, Lord Tennyson (1809–92)

The Lady of Shalott [extracts]

Many generations of school children have memorized this poem, with the help of its irresistible singsong rhythm.

On either side the river lie
Long fields of barley and of rye,
That clothe the wold and meet the sky;
And thro' the field the road runs by
To many-towered Camelot;
And up and down the people go,
Gazing where the lilies blow
Round an island there below,
The island of Shalott.

Willows whiten, aspens quiver,
Little breezes dusk and shiver
Thro' the wave that runs for ever
By the island in the river
Flowing down to Camelot.
Four grey walls, and four grey towers,
Overlook a space of flowers,
And the silent isle imbowers
The Lady of Shalott.

By the margin, willow veiled
Slide the heavy barges trailed
By slow horses; and unhailed
The shallop flitteth silken-sailed
Skimming down to Camelot:
But who hath seen her wave her hand?
Or at the casement seen her stand?
Or is she known in all the land,
The Lady of Shalott?

Only reapers, reaping early
In among the bearded barley,
Hear a song that echoes cheerly
From the river winding clearly,
Down to towered Camelot:
And by the moon the reaper weary,
Piling sheaves in uplands airy,
Listening, whispers, ''Tis the fairy
Lady of Shalott.'

There she weaves by night and day
A magic web with colours gay.
She has heard a whisper say,
A curse is on her if she stay

To look down to Camelot.
She knows not what the curse may be,
And so she weaveth steadily,
And little other care hath she,
The Lady of Shalott.

. . .

His broad clear brow in sunlight glowed;
On burnished hooves his war-horse trode;
From underneath his helmet flowed
His coal-black curls as on he rode,
As he rode down to Camelot.
From the bank and from the river
He flashed into the crystal mirror,
'Tirra lirra,' by the river
Sang Sir Lancelot.

She left the web, she left the loom,
She made three paces thro' the room,
She saw the water-lily bloom,
She saw the helmet and the plume,
She looked down to Camelot.
Out flew the web and floated wide;
The mirror cracked from side to side;
'The curse is come upon me,' cried
The Lady of Shalott.

Anne Sexton (1928–74)

Her Kind

I have gone out, a possessed witch,
haunting the black air, braver at night;
dreaming evil, I have done my hitch
over the plain houses, light by light:
lonely thing, twelve-fingered, out of mind.
A woman like that is not a woman, quite.
I have been her kind.

I have found the warm caves in the woods,
filled them with skillets, carvings, shelves,
closets, silks, innumerable goods;
fixed the suppers for the worms and the elves:
whining, rearranging the disaligned.
A woman like that is misunderstood.
I have been her kind.

I have ridden in your cart, driver,
waved my nude arms at villages going by,
learning the last bright routes, survivor
where your flames still bite my thigh
and my ribs crack where your wheels wind.
A woman like that is not ashamed to die.
I have been her kind.

Walter De la Mare (1873–1956)

The Listeners

This poem leaves so many questions unanswered: who is the Traveller? What vow had he sworn? Who are the throng of ghostly listeners? In learning it, you are absorbing the heart of countless possible stories.

'Is there anybody there?' said the Traveller,
Knocking on the moonlit door;
And his horse in the silence champed the grasses
Of the forest's ferny floor:
And a bird flew up out of the turret,
Above the Traveller's head:
And he smote upon the door again a second time;
'Is there anybody there?' he said.
But no one descended to the Traveller;
No head from the leaf-fringed sill
Leaned over and looked into his grey eyes,
Where he stood perplexed and still.
But only a host of phantom listeners
That dwelt in the lone house then
Stood listening in the quiet of the moonlight
To that voice from the world of men:
Stood thronging the faint moonbeams on the dark stair,
That goes down to the empty hall,
Hearkening in an air stirr'd and shaken
By the lonely Traveller's call.
And he felt in his heart their strangeness,
Their stillness answering his cry,
While his horse moved, cropping the dark turf,
'Neath the starred and leafy sky;

For he suddenly smote on the door, even
Louder, and lifted his head:–
'Tell them I came, and no one answered,
That I kept my word,' he said.
Never the least stir made the listeners,
Though every word he spake
Fell echoing through the shadowiness of the still house
From the one man left awake:
Ay, they heard his foot upon the stirrup,
And the sound of iron on stone,
And how the silence surged softly backward,
When the plunging hoofs were gone.

Edgar Allen Poe (1809–49)

The Raven [extracts]

Once upon a midnight dreary, while I pondered, weak and weary,
Over many a quaint and curious volume of forgotten lore—
While I nodded, nearly napping, suddenly there came a tapping,
As of some one gently rapping, rapping at my chamber door.
''Tis some visitor,' I muttered, 'tapping at my chamber door—
Only this and nothing more.'

Ah, distinctly I remember it was in the bleak December;
And each separate dying ember wrought its ghost upon the floor.
Eagerly I wished the morrow;—vainly I had sought to borrow
From my books surcease of sorrow—sorrow for the lost Lenore—
For the rare and radiant maiden whom the angels name Lenore—
Nameless *here* for evermore.

. . .

And the silken, sad, uncertain rustling of each purple curtain
Thrilled me—filled me with fantastic terrors never felt before;
So that now, to still the beating of my heart, I stood repeating
''Tis some visiter entreating entrance at my chamber door—
Some late visitor entreating entrance at my chamber door;—
                    This it is and nothing more.'

. . .

Open here I flung the shutter, when, with many a flirt and flutter,
In there stepped a stately Raven of the saintly days of yore;
Not the least obeisance made he; not a minute stopped or stayed he;
But, with mien of lord or lady, perched above my chamber door—
Perched upon a bust of Pallas just above my chamber door—
                  Perched, and sat, and nothing more.

. . .

'Prophet!' said I, 'thing of evil!—prophet still, if bird or devil!—
By that Heaven that bends above us—by that God we both adore—
Tell this soul with sorrow laden if, within the distant Aidenn,
It shall clasp a sainted maiden whom the angels name Lenore—
Clasp a rare and radiant maiden whom the angels name Lenore.'
                  Quoth the Raven, 'Nevermore.'

'Be that word our sign of parting, bird or fiend!,' I shrieked, upstarting—
'Get thee back into the tempest and the Night's Plutonian shore!
Leave no black plume as a token of that lie thy soul hath spoken!
Leave my loneliness unbroken!—quit the bust above my door!
Take thy beak from out my heart, and take thy form from off my door!'
                  Quoth the Raven, 'Nevermore.'

And the Raven, never flitting, still is sitting, *still* is sitting
On the pallid bust of Pallas just above my chamber door;
And his eyes have all the seeming of a demon's that is dreaming,
And the lamp-light o'er him streaming throws his shadow on the floor;
And my soul from out that shadow that lies floating on the floor
                                        Shall be lifted—nevermore!

'Always learn poems by heart. They have to become the marrow in your bones. Like fluoride in the water, they'll make your soul impervious to the world's soft decay.'

Janet Fitch, *White Oleander*

Two

Sunward I've climbed: Adventure

Poetry is designed for more than just moments of tranquillity. The following verses of action and drama, of voyages through the sea and sky, can inspire and provide secret pleasure in an everyday world that is, sometimes, not as full of ripping yarns as we might like.

Lord George Gordon Byron (1788–1824)

The Destruction of Sennacherib

The Assyrian came down like the wolf on the fold,
    And his cohorts were gleaming in purple and gold;
    And the sheen of their spears was like stars on the sea,
    When the blue wave rolls nightly on deep Galilee.

Like the leaves of the forest when Summer is green,
    That host with their banners at sunset were seen:
    Like the leaves of the forest when autumn hath blown,
    That host on the morrow lay withered and strown.

For the Angel of Death spread his wings on the blast,
    And breathed in the face of the foe as he passed;
    And the eyes of the sleepers waxed deadly and chill,
    And their hearts but once heaved, and for ever grew still!

And there lay the steed with his nostril all wide,
    But through it there rolled not the breath of his pride;
    And the foam of his gasping lay white on the turf,
    And cold as the spray of the rock-beating surf.

And there lay the rider distorted and pale,
    With the dew on his brow, and the rust on his mail:
    And the tents were all silent, the banners alone,
    The lances unlifted, the trumpet unblown.

And the widows of Ashur are loud in their wail,
    And the idols are broke in the temple of Baal;
    And the might of the Gentile, unsmote by the sword,
    Hath melted like snow in the glance of the Lord!

Samuel Taylor Coleridge (1772–1834)

The Rime of the Ancient Mariner [extracts]

*Passages from this poem – including 'Water, water, everywhere /
Nor any drop to drink' and 'I blessed them unaware' – clutch at
the memory. The mariner's ballad has a hypnotic rhythm that
makes it easy to learn, though the full version is long and would
be a fantastic challenge.*

It is an ancient Mariner,
And he stoppeth one of three.
'By thy long grey beard and glittering eye,
Now wherefore stopp'st thou me?

The Bridegroom's doors are opened wide,
And I am next of kin;
The guests are met, the feast is set:
May'st hear the merry din.'

He holds him with his skinny hand,
'There was a ship,' quoth he.
'Hold off! unhand me, grey-beard loon!'
Eftsoons his hand dropt he.

He holds him with his glittering eye—
The Wedding-Guest stood still,
And listens like a three years' child:
The Mariner hath his will.

. . .

Day after day, day after day,
We stuck, nor breath nor motion;
As idle as a painted ship

Upon a painted ocean.

Water, water, every where,
And all the boards did shrink;
Water, water, every where,
Nor any drop to drink.

The very deep did rot: O Christ!
That ever this should be!
Yea, slimy things did crawl with legs
Upon the slimy sea.

About, about, in reel and rout
The death-fires danced at night;
The water, like a witch's oils,
Burnt green, and blue and white.

And some in dreams assurèd were
Of the Spirit that plagued us so;
Nine fathom deep he had followed us
From the land of mist and snow.

And every tongue, through utter drought,
Was withered at the root;
We could not speak, no more than if
We had been choked with soot.

Ah! well-a-day! what evil looks
Had I from old and young!
Instead of the cross, the Albatross
About my neck was hung.

. . .

Farewell, farewell! but this I tell
To thee, thou Wedding-Guest!

He prayeth well, who loveth well
Both man and bird and beast.

He prayeth best, who loveth best
All things both great and small;
For the dear God who loveth us,
He made and loveth all.

The Mariner, whose eye is bright,
Whose beard with age is hoar,
Is gone; and now the Wedding-Guest
Turned from the bridegroom's door.

He went like one that hath been stunned,
And is of sense forlorn:
A sadder and a wiser man,
He rose the morrow morn.

John Masefield (1878–1967)

Sea-Fever

I must down to the seas again, to the lonely sea and the sky,
And all I ask is a tall ship and a star to steer her by,
And the wheel's kick and the wind's song
    and the white sail's shaking,
And a grey mist on the sea's face and a grey dawn breaking.

I must down to the seas again, for the call of the running tide
Is a wild call and a clear call that may not be denied;
And all I ask is a windy day with the white clouds flying,
And the flung spray and the blown spume,
    and the sea-gulls crying.

I must down to the seas again, to the vagrant gypsy life,
To the gull's way and the whale's way where
    the wind's like a whetted knife;
And all I ask is a merry yarn from a laughing fellow-rover,
And quiet sleep and a sweet dream when the long trick's over.

John Gillespie Magee (1922–41)

High Flight

Oh, I have slipped the surly bonds of earth
And danced the skies on laughter-silvered wings;
Sunward I've climbed, and joined the tumbling mirth
Of sun-split clouds, – and done a hundred things
You have not dreamed of, – wheeled and soared and swung
High in the sunlit silence. Hov'ring there,
I've chased the shouting wind along, and flung
My eager craft through footless halls of air . . .
Up, up the long, delirious, burning blue
I've topped the windswept heights with easy grace
Where never lark, or even eagle flew –
And, while with silent, lifting mind I've trod
The high untrespassed sanctity of space,
Put out my hand, and touched the face of God.

Three

From antique lands to Berkshire: On the Move

The rhythm of a poem can convey great movement, as well as providing you with a tool to remember certain lines. Take W.H. Auden's 'Night Mail', which guides you expertly through the gentle to and fro of a train journey. Whether you are on the road to far-flung lands or simply to the much-maligned town of Slough, drawing upon a poem or two from your memory can help the miles speed by.

W.H. Auden (1907–73)

Night Mail

The fantastic chugging rhythm of this poem makes it both easy to recall and hugely evocative when recited aloud.

This is the Night Mail crossing the Border,
Bringing the cheque and the postal order,

Letters for the rich, letters for the poor,
The shop at the corner, the girl next door.

Pulling up Beattock, a steady climb:
The gradient's against her, but she's on time.

Past cotton-grass and moorland boulder
Shovelling white steam over her shoulder,

Snorting noisily, she passes
Silent miles of wind-bent grasses.

Birds turn their heads as she approaches,
Stare from bushes at her blank-faced coaches.

Sheep-dogs cannot turn her course;
They slumber on with paws across.

In the farm she passes no one wakes,
But a jug in a bedroom gently shakes.

Dawn freshens. Her climb is done.
Down towards Glasgow she descends,
Towards the steam tugs yelping down a glade of cranes,
Towards the fields of apparatus, the furnaces
Set on the dark plain like gigantic chessmen.
All Scotland waits for her:

In dark glens, beside pale-green lochs,
Men long for news.

Letters of thanks, letters from banks,
Letters of joy from girl and boy,
Receipted bills and invitations
To inspect new stock or to visit relations,
And applications for situations,
And timid lovers' declarations,
And gossip, gossip from all the nations,
News circumstantial, news financial,
Letters with holiday snaps to enlarge in,
Letters with faces scrawled on the margin,
Letters from uncles, cousins and aunts,
Letters to Scotland from the South of France,
Letters of condolence to Highlands and Lowlands,
Written on paper of every hue,
The pink, the violet, the white and the blue,
The chatty, the catty, the boring, the adoring,
The cold and official and the heart's outpouring,
Clever, stupid, short and long,
The typed and the printed and the spelt all wrong.

Thousands are still asleep,
Dreaming of terrifying monsters
Or of friendly tea beside the band in Cranston's or Crawford's:
Asleep in working Glasgow, asleep in well-set Edinburgh,
Asleep in granite Aberdeen,
They continue their dreams,
But shall wake soon and hope for letters,
And none will hear the postman's knock
Without a quickening of the heart.
For who can bear to feel himself forgotten?

Robert Browning (1812–89)

Home-Thoughts, from Abroad

Oh, to be in England
Now that April's there,
And whoever wakes in England
Sees, some morning, unaware,
That the lowest boughs and the brushwood sheaf
Round the elm-tree bole are in tiny leaf,
While the chaffinch sings on the orchard bough
In England—now!

And after April, when May follows,
And the whitethroat builds, and all the swallows!
Hark, where my blossomed pear-tree in the hedge
Leans to the field and scatters on the clover
Blossoms and dewdrops—at the bent spray's edge—
That's the wise thrush; he sings each song twice over,
Lest you should think he never could recapture
The first fine careless rapture!
And though the fields look rough with hoary dew,
All will be gay when noontide wakes anew
The buttercups, the little children's dower
—Far brighter than this gaudy melon-flower!

John Betjeman (1906–84)

Slough

Betjeman's much loved poems tend to be easy to learn and fun to recite – though the denizens of Slough might not thank you.

Come, friendly bombs, and fall on Slough!
It isn't fit for humans now,
There isn't grass to graze a cow
Swarm over, Death!

Come, bombs, and blow to smithereens
Those air-conditioned, bright canteens,
Tinned fruit, tinned meat, tinned milk, tinned beans,
Tinned minds, tinned breath.

Mess up the mess they call a town–
A house for ninety-seven down
And once a week a half-a-crown
For twenty years,

And get that man with double chin
Who'll always cheat and always win,
Who washes his repulsive skin
In women's tears,

And smash his desk of polished oak
And smash his hands so used to stroke
And stop his boring dirty joke
And make him yell.

But spare the bald young clerks who add
The profits of the stinking cad;
It's not their fault that they are mad,

They've tasted Hell.

It's not their fault they do not know
The birdsong from the radio,
It's not their fault they often go
To Maidenhead

And talk of sport and makes of cars
In various bogus Tudor bars
And daren't look up and see the stars
But belch instead.

In labour-saving homes, with care
Their wives frizz out peroxide hair
And dry it in synthetic air
And paint their nails.

Come, friendly bombs, and fall on Slough
To get it ready for the plough.
The cabbages are coming now;
The earth exhales.

Robert Louis Stevenson (1850–94)

From a Railway Carriage

Here is another hymn to the railway that demands a speedy recitation due to its driving rhythm.

Faster than fairies, faster than witches,
Bridges and houses, hedges and ditches;
And charging along like troops in a battle
All through the meadows the horses and cattle:
All of the sights of the hill and the plain

Fly as thick as driving rain;
And ever again, in the wink of an eye,
Painted stations whistle by.
Here is a child who clambers and scrambles,
All by himself and gathering brambles;
Here is a tramp who stands and gazes;
And here is the green for stringing the daisies!
Here is a cart runaway in the road
Lumping along with man and load;
And here is a mill, and there is a river:
Each a glimpse and gone forever!

Howard Moss (1922–87)

Tourists

Moss's cutting poem contains some stunning rhymes, notably the lovely 'embarrassed in Paris'. Should you be subjected to dreary travellers' tales, it's a naughty treat to revisit these lines mentally as your captors reach for the photographs.

Cramped like sardines on the Queens, and sedated,
The sittings all first, the roommates mismated,

Three nuns at the table, the waiter a barber,
Then dumped with their luggage at some frumpish harbor,

Veering through rapids in a vapid *rapido*
To view the new moon from a ruin on the Lido,

Or a sundown in London from a rundown Mercedes, Then
high-borne to Glynebourne for Orfeo in Hades,

Embarrassed in Paris in Harris tweed, dying to
Get to the next museum piece that they're flying to,

Finding, in Frankfurt, the one indigestible
Comestible makes them too ill for the Festival,

Footloose in Lucerne, or taking a pub in in
Stratford or Glasgow, or maudlin in Dublin, in-

sensitive, garrulous, querulous, audible,
Drunk in the Dolomites, tuning a portable,

Homesick in Stockholm, or dressed to toboggan
At the wrong time of year in too dear Copenhagen,

Generally being too genial or hostile—
Too grand at the Grand, too old at the Hostel—

Humdrum conundrums, what's to become of them?
Most will come home, but there will be some of them

Subsiding like Lawrence in Florence, or crazily
Ending up tending shop up in Fiesole.

Emma Lazarus (1849–87)

The New Colossus

*Lazarus's verse is inspired by New York's Statue of Liberty, and
was written to raise funds for its pedestal.*

Not like the brazen giant of Greek fame,
With conquering limbs astride from land to land;
Here at our sea-washed, sunset gates shall stand
A mighty woman with a torch, whose flame
Is the imprisoned lightning, and her name

Mother of Exiles. From her beacon-hand
Glows world-wide welcome; her mild eyes command.
The air-bridged harbor that twin cities frame.
'Keep, ancient lands, your storied pomp!' cries she
With silent lips. 'Give me your tired, your poor,
Your huddled masses yearning to breathe free,
The wretched refuse of your teeming shore.
Send these, the homeless, tempest-tosst to me,
I lift my lamp beside the golden door!'

Percy Bysshe Shelley (1792–1822)

Ozymandias

I met a traveller from an antique land
Who said: Two vast and trunkless legs of stone
Stand in the desert. Near them, on the sand,
Half sunk, a shattered visage lies, whose frown,
And wrinkled lip, and sneer of cold command,
Tell that its sculptor well those passions read
Which yet survive, stamped on these lifeless things,
The hand that mocked them and the heart that fed.
And on the pedestal these words appear:
'My name is Ozymandias, king of kings:
Look on my works, ye Mighty, and despair!'
Nothing beside remains. Round the decay
Of that colossal wreck, boundless and bare
The lone and level sands stretch far away.

'The future of the humanities as a common possession depends on the restoration of a simple, single ideal: getting poetry by heart.'

Clive James, *Cultural Amnesia*

Four

Let us be true to one another: Love

From the heady days of early romance to the pain of unrequited
affection, the vagaries of love have been captured by some of our
greatest poets. Romantic verse finds its way into our love letters –
or perhaps love emails, nowadays – and wedding services, because
poetry can speak with an eloquence we tend to lack. Whether in
search of the right way in which to express your feelings for the
object of your ardour, or simply a line to sum up the pain of a lost
love, this collection of beautiful poetry is worth memorizing.

Ben Jonson (*c.*1572–1637)

Song: to Celia

Drink to me only with thine eyes,
And I will pledge with mine;
Or leave a kiss but in the cup,
And I'll not look for wine.
The thirst that from the soul doth rise
Doth ask a drink divine:
But might I of Jove's nectar sup,
I would not change for thine.

I sent thee late a rosy wreath,
Not so much honouring thee,
As giving it a hope that there
It could not withered be.
But thou thereon didst only breathe,
And sent'st it back to me;
Since when it grows and smells, I swear,
Not of itself, but thee.

Matthew Arnold (1822–88)

Dover Beach

This is not the easiest of poems to learn because its rhythm runs in tidal swirls and eddies. But there is a mysterious loveliness to it that repays the effort.

The sea is calm to-night.
The tide is full, the moon lies fair
Upon the straits; – on the French coast the light

Gleams and is gone; the cliffs of England stand,
Glimmering and vast, out in the tranquil bay.
Come to the window, sweet is the night-air!

Only, from the long line of spray
Where the sea meets the moon-blanch'd land,
Listen! you hear the grating roar
Of pebbles which the waves draw back, and fling,
At their return, up the high strand,
Begin, and cease, and then again begin,
With tremulous cadence slow, and bring
The eternal note of sadness in.

Sophocles long ago
Heard it on the Ægæan, and it brought
Into his mind the turbid ebb and flow
Of human misery; we
Find also in the sound a thought,
Hearing it by this distant northern sea.

The Sea of Faith
Was once, too, at the full, and round earth's shore
Lay like the folds of a bright girdle furl'd.
But now I only hear
Its melancholy, long, withdrawing roar,
Retreating, to the breath
Of the night-wind, down the vast edges drear
And naked shingles of the world.

Ah, love, let us be true
To one another! for the world, which seems
To lie before us like a land of dreams,
So various, so beautiful, so new,
Hath really neither joy, nor love, nor light,

Nor certitude, nor peace, nor help for pain;
And we are here as on a darkling plain
Swept with confused alarms of struggle and flight,
Where ignorant armies clash by night.

Elizabeth Barrett Browning (1806–61)

Sonnet 43 'How do I love thee?'

How do I love thee? Let me count the ways.
I love thee to the depth and breadth and height
My soul can reach, when feeling out of sight
For the ends of Being and ideal Grace.
I love thee to the level of everyday's
Most quiet need, by sun and candle-light.
I love thee freely, as men strive for Right;
I love thee purely, as they turn from Praise.
I love thee with the passion put to use
In my old griefs, and with my childhood's faith.
I love thee with a love I seemed to lose
With my lost saints,—I love thee with the breath,
Smiles, tears, of all my life!—and, if God choose,
I shall but love thee better after death.

Robert Herrick (1591–1674)

To the Virgins, To Make Much of Time

Herrick's verses have a rapid pace to remind us how quickly time passes.

Gather ye rosebuds while ye may,
Old Time is still a-flying;
And this same flower that smiles today,
Tomorrow will be dying.

The glorious lamp of heaven, the sun,
The higher he's a-getting,
The sooner will his race be run,
And nearer he's to setting.

That age is best which is the first,
When youth and blood are warmer;
But being spent, the worse, and worst
Times, still succeed the former.

Then be not coy, but use your time,
And while ye may, go marry;
For having lost but once your prime,
You may forever tarry.

Andrew Marvell (1621–78)

To His Coy Mistress

Marvell's poem repeats the sentiment of Herrick's: young ladies shouldn't withhold their affections from their ardent lovers. However, it is more of a challenge to commit to memory than Herrick's. The famous phrase concerning 'Time's winged chariot' and its hurrying will often spring to the mind of the busy.

Had we but World enough, and Time,
This coyness, Lady, were no crime.
We would sit down, and think which way
To walk, and pass our long Loves Day.
Thou by the *Indian Ganges* side
Should'st Rubies find: I by the Tide
Of *Humber* would complain. I would
Love you ten years before the Flood:
And you should if you please refuse
Till the conversion of the *Jews*.
My vegetable Love should grow
Vaster than Empires, and more slow.
An hundred years should go to praise
Thine Eyes, and on thy Forehead Gaze.
Two hundred to adore each Breast:
But thirty thousand to the rest.
An Age at least to every part,
And the last Age should show your Heart.
For Lady, you deserve this State;
Nor would I love at lower rate.
　　But at my back I alwaies hear
Times wingèd Charriot hurrying near:
And yonder all before us lye

Desarts of vast Eternity.
Thy Beauty shall no more be found;
Nor, in thy marble Vault, shall sound
My ecchoing Song: then Worms shall try
That long preserv'd Virginity:
And your quaint Honour turn to dust;
And into ashes all my Lust.
The Grave's a fine and private place,
But none, I think, do there embrace.

   Now therefore, while the youthful hew
Sits on thy skin like morning dew,
And while thy willing Soul transpires
At every pore with instant Fires,
Now let us sport us while we may;
And now, like am'rous birds of prey,
Rather at once our Time devour,
Than languish in his slow-chapt pow'r.
Let us roll all our Strength, and all
Our sweetness, up into one Ball:
And tear our Pleasure with rough strife.
Through the Iron gates of Life.
Thus, though we cannot make our Sun
Stand still, yet we will make him run.

Wendy Cope (1945–)

Valentine

My heart has made its mind up
And I'm afraid it's you.
Whatever you've got lined up,
My heart has made its mind up
And if you can't be signed up
This year, next year will do.
My heart has made its mind up
And I'm afraid it's you.

Thomas Campion (1567–1620)

There is a Garden in her Face

There is a garden in her face,
Where roses and white lilies grow,
A heavenly paradise is that place,
Wherein all pleasant fruits do flow.
There cherries grow which none may buy
Till 'Cherry ripe!' themselves do cry.

Those cherries fairly do enclose
Of orient pearl a double row,
Which when her lovely laughter shows,
They look like rose-buds filled with snow.
Yet them nor peer nor prince can buy,
Till 'Cherry ripe!' themselves do cry.

Her eyes like angels watch them still;
Her brows like bended bows do stand,
Threatening with piercing frowns to kill

All that attempt with eye or hand
Those sacred cherries to come nigh,
Till 'Cherry ripe!' themselves do cry.

Anne Bradstreet (1612–72)

To My Dear and Loving Husband

If ever two were one, then surely we.
If ever man were loved by wife, then thee;
If ever wife was happy in a man,
Compare with me ye women if you can.
I prize thy love more than whole mines of gold,
Or all the riches that the East doth hold.
My love is such that rivers cannot quench,
Nor ought but love from thee give recompense.
Thy love is such I can no way repay;
The heavens reward thee manifold, I pray.
Then while we live, in love let's so persever,
That when we live no more we may live ever.

Robert Herrick (1591–1674)

Delight in Disorder

Here's a sweet and slightly saucy poem for you gentlemen to keep up your sleeves for those times when your beloved decides she looks 'a mess'.

A sweet disorder in the dresse
Kindles in cloathes a wantonnesse:
A Lawne about the shoulders thrown

Into a fine distraction:
An erring Lace, which here and there
Enthralls the Crimson Stomacher:
A Cuffe neglectfull, and thereby
Ribbands to flow confusedly:
A winning wave (deserving Note)
In the tempestuous petticote:
A careless shoe-string, in whose tye
I see a wilde civility:
Do more bewitch me, than when Art
Is too precise in every part.

Christina Rossetti (1830–94)

A Birthday

My heart is like a singing bird
Whose nest is in a water'd shoot;
My heart is like an apple tree
Whose boughs are bent with thickset fruit;
My heart is like a rainbow shell
That paddles in a halcyon sea;
My heart is gladder than all these
Because my love is come to me.

Raise me a dais of silk and down;
Hang it with vair and purple dyes;
Carve it in doves and pomegranates,
And peacocks with a hundred eyes;
Work it in gold and silver grapes,
In leaves and silver fleurs-de-lys;
Because the birthday of my life
Is come, my love is come to me.

William Shakespeare (1564–1616)

Sonnet 116

This is a marvellous choice for a wedding reading. The beauty of this sonnet is that it is not written in the first person, which means it can be read by a favourite aunt without her sounding as if she's declaring her passion for the groom. It also expounds an appropriate sentiment: you lovebirds have happily made your bed – now you must lie in it!

Let me not to the marriage of true mindes
Admit impediments, love is not love
Which alters when it alteration findes,
Or bends with the remover to remove.
O no, it is an ever fixèd marke
That lookes on tempests and is never shaken;
It is the star to every wandring barke,
Whose worths unknowne, although his height be taken.
Lov's not Times foole, though rosie lips and cheeks
Within his bending sickles compasse come,
Love alters not with his breef houres and weekes,
But beares it out even to the edge of doome
    If this be error and upon me proved,
    I never writ, nor no man ever loved.

William Shakespeare (1564–1616)

Sonnet 130

My Mistres eyes are nothing like the Sunne,
Corrall is farre more red, than her lips red,
If snow be white, why then her brests are dun:
If haires be wiers, black wiers grow on her head:
I have seene Roses damaskt, red and white,
But no such Roses see I in her cheekes,
And in some perfumes is there more delight,
Than in the breath that from my Mistres reekes.
I love to heare her speake, yet well I know,
That Musicke hath a farre more pleasing sound:
I graunt I never saw a goddesse goe,
My Mistres when shee walkes treads on the ground.
    And yet by heaven I thinke my love as rare,
    As any she beli'd with false compare.

Carol Ann Duffy (1955–)

Anne Hathaway

The bed we loved in was a spinning world
of forests, castles, torchlight, clifftops, seas
where he would dive for pearls. My lover's words
were shooting stars which fell to earth as kisses
on these lips; my body now a softer rhyme
to his, now echo, assonance; his touch
a verb dancing in the centre of a noun.
Some nights, I dreamed he'd written me, the bed
a page beneath his writer's hands. Romance
and drama played by touch, by scent, by taste.

In the other bed, the best, our guests dozed on,
dribbling their prose. My living laughing love—
I hold him in the casket of my widow's head
as he held me upon that next best bed.

John Donne (1572–1631)

The Good-Morrow

I wonder, by my troth, what thou and I
Did, till we loved? were we not weaned till then ?
But sucked on country pleasures, childishly?
Or snorted we in the Seven Sleepers' den?
'Twas so; but this, all pleasures fancies be.
If ever any beauty I did see,
Which I desired, and got, 'twas but a dream of thee.
And now good-morrow to our waking souls,
Which watch not one another out of fear;
For love, all love of other sights controls,
And makes one little room an everywhere.
Let sea-discoverers to new worlds have gone,
Let maps to others, worlds on worlds have shown,
Let us possess one world; each hath one, and is one.

My face in thine eye, thine in mine appears,
And true plain hearts do in the faces rest;
Where can we find two better hemispheres
Without sharp North, without declining West?
Whatever dies, was not mixed equally;
If our two loves be one, or, thou and I
Love so alike that none do slacken, none can die.

W.B. Yeats (1865–1939)

Aedh Wishes for the Cloths of Heaven

Had I the heavens' embroidered cloths,
Enwrought with golden and silver light,
The blue and the dim and the dark cloths
Of night and light and the half light,
I would spread the cloths under your feet:
But I, being poor, have only my dreams;
I have spread my dreams under your feet;
Tread softly because you tread on my dreams.

Five

Stooping to folly: Love Songs for Cynics

As any poet knows, the course of true love does not always run smoothly, which means they have not shied away from immortalizing tawdry betrayals, the rancour of previously enamoured suitors and the cruelty of unrequited passion. No doubt composing these bitter verses served as an excellent catharsis – just as reciting them can be a balm to the disappointed in love. The cynic could argue that more true wisdom lies in these poems than in those that made up the preceding chapter, but that will depend on your own point of view.

Louise Bogan (1897–1970)

Juan's Song

When beauty breaks and falls asunder
I feel no grief for it, but wonder.
When love, like a frail shell, lies broken,
I keep no chip of it for token.
I never had a man for friend
Who did not know that love must end.
I never had a girl for lover
Who could discern when love was over.
What the wise doubt, the fool believes—
Who is it, then, that love deceives?

Robert Browning (1812–89)

My Last Duchess

Although this poem is often prescribed for learning, the structure is not simple and the sentiment scathing. Anyone who can intimately recall it, though, seems to cherish great affection for the Duke's reminiscences about his spirited Duchess.

That's my last Duchess painted on the wall,
Looking as if she were alive. I call
That piece a wonder, now: Frà Pandolf's hands
Worked busily a day, and there she stands.
Will't please you sit and look at her? I said
'Frà Pandolf' by design, for never read
Strangers like you that pictured countenance,
The depth and passion of its earnest glance,
But to myself they turned (since none puts by

The curtain I have drawn for you, but I)
And seemed as they would ask me, if they durst,
How such a glance came there; so, not the first
Are you to turn and ask thus. Sir, 't was not
Her husband's presence only, called that spot
Of joy into the Duchess' cheek: perhaps
Frà Pandolf chanced to say 'Her mantle laps
Over my lady's wrist too much,' or 'Paint
Must never hope to reproduce the faint
Half-flush that dies along her throat': such stuff
Was courtesy, she thought, and cause enough
For calling up that spot of joy. She had
A heart — how shall I say? — too soon made glad,
Too easily impressed; she liked whate'er
She looked on, and her looks went everywhere.
Sir, 't was all one! My favour at her breast,
The dropping of the daylight in the West,
The bough of cherries some officious fool
Broke in the orchard for her, the white mule
She rode with round the terrace — all and each
Would draw from her alike the approving speech,
Or blush, at least. She thanked men, — good! but thanked
Somehow — I know not how — as if she ranked
My gift of a nine-hundred-years-old name
With anybody's gift. Who'd stoop to blame
This sort of trifling? Even had you skill
In speech — (which I have not) — to make your will
Quite clear to such an one, and say, 'Just this
Or that in you disgusts me; here you miss,
Or there exceed the mark' — and if she let
Herself be lessoned so, nor plainly set
Her wits to yours, forsooth, and made excuse,

—E'en then would be some stooping; and I choose
Never to stoop. Oh sir, she smiled, no doubt,
Whene'er I passed her; but who passed without
Much the same smile? This grew; I gave commands;
Then all smiles stopped together. There she stands
As if alive. Will't please you rise? We'll meet
The company below, then. I repeat,
The Count your master's known munificence
Is ample warrant that no just pretence
Of mine for dowry will be disallowed;
Though his fair daughter's self, as I avowed
At starting, is my object. Nay, we'll go
Together down, sir. Notice Neptune, though,
Taming a sea-horse, thought a rarity,
Which Claus of Innsbruck cast in bronze for me!

Oliver Goldsmith (c.1730–74)

When Lovely Woman Stoops to Folly

When lovely woman stoops to folly,
    And finds too late that men betray,
What charm can soothe her melancholy,
    What art can wash her guilt away?

The only art her guilt to cover,
    To hide her shame from every eye,
To give repentance to her lover,
    And wring his bosom, is—to die.

Philip Bourke Marston (1850–87)

Love's Warfare

'And are these cold, light words your last?' he said,
And rose, his face made pale with outraged love.
She answered gaily, 'Are they not enough?'
And lightly laughed until his spirit bled,
While snake-like on his grief her beauty fed.
He looked upon her face once more for proof,
Then through and through his lips the sharp teeth drove,
Till with the bitter dew of blood made red.
At length he said, 'And so 'twas but a jest,
A well-conceived, well-executed plan;
Yet now may God forgive you, if God can!'
And, passing, left her calm and self-possessed.
She watched him cross the lawn with eyes bent low,
Where she had kissed his face one hour ago.

Dorothy Parker (1893–1967)

The Lady's Reward

Lady, lady, never start
Conversation toward your heart;
Keep your pretty words serene;
Never murmur what you mean.
Show yourself, by word and look,
Swift and shallow as a brook.
Be as cool and quick to go
As a drop of April snow;
Be as delicate and gay
As a cherry flower in May.

Lady, lady, never speak
Of the tears that burn your cheek–
She will never win him, whose
Words had shown she feared to lose.
Be you wise and never sad,
You will get your lovely lad.
Never serious be, nor true,
And your wish will come to you–
And if that makes you happy, kid,
You'll be the first it ever did.

A.E. Housman (1859–1936)

When I Was One-and-Twenty

When I was one-and-twenty
I heard a wise man say,
'Give crowns and pounds and guineas
But not your heart away;
Give pearls away and rubies
But keep your fancy free.'
But I was one-and-twenty,
No use to talk to me.

When I was one-and-twenty
I heard him say again,
'The heart out of the bosom
Was never given in vain;
'Tis paid with sighs a plenty
And sold for endless rue.'
And I am two-and-twenty,
And oh, 'tis true, 'tis true.

Lord George Gordon Byron (1788–1824)

When We Two Parted

These are vicious verses for the disappointed in love.

When we two parted
 In silence and tears,
Half broken-hearted
 To sever for years,
Pale grew thy cheek and cold,
 Colder thy kiss;
Truly that hour foretold
 Sorrow to this.

The dew of the morning
 Sank chill on my brow—
It felt like the warning
 Of what I feel now.
Thy vows are all broken,
 And light is thy fame:
I hear thy name spoken,
 And share in its shame.

They name thee before me,
 A knell to mine ear;
A shudder comes o'er me—
 Why wert thou so dear?
They know not I knew thee,
 Who knew thee too well:
Long, long shall I rue thee,
 Too deeply to tell.

In secret we met—
    In silence I grieve,
That thy heart could forget,
    Thy spirit deceive.
If I should meet thee
    After long years,
How should I greet thee?
    With silence and tears.

Dante Gabriel Rossetti (1828–82)

Jenny [extract]

Rossetti certainly had an eye for the ladies, hence this slightly misty-eyed celebration of a good-time girl.

Lazy laughing languid Jenny,
Fond of a kiss and fond of a guinea,
Whose head upon my knee to-night
Rests for a while, as if grown light
With all our dances and the sound
To which the wild tunes spun you round:
Fair Jenny mine, the thoughtless queen
Of kisses which the blush between
Could hardly make much daintier;
Whose eyes are as blue skies, whose hair
Is countless gold incomparable:
Fresh flower, scarce touched with signs that tell
Of Love's exuberant hotbed:–Nay,
Poor flower left torn since yesterday
Until to-morrow leave you bare;
Poor handful of bright spring-water

Flung in the whirlpool's shrieking face;
Poor shameful Jenny, full of grace
Thus with your head upon my knee;–
Whose person or whose purse may be
The lodestar of your reverie?

Elizabeth Siddal (1829–62)

The Lust of the Eyes

Rossetti's long-suffering lover and, later, wife knew more than most about men who worshipped beauty.

I care not for my Lady's soul,
Though I worship before her smile:
I care not where be my Lady's goal
When her beauty shall lose its wile.

Low sit I down at my Lady's feet,
Gazing through her wild eyes,
Smiling to think how my love will fleet
When their starlike beauty dies.

I care not if my Lady pray
To our Father which is in Heaven;
But for joy my heart's quick pulses play,
For to me her love is given.

Then who shall close my Lady's eyes,
And who shall fold her hands?
Will any hearken if she cries
Up to the unknown lands?

'Poetry is all that is worth remembering in life.'

William Hazlitt

Six

The poison-swellëd snake: Anger

Conjuring up hate-filled encounters and friendships torn apart by deceit, the poems in this chapter speak of bitterness and betrayal, anger and wrath, and provide the reader with a stinging line or two to recite when the need might arise. You might also find it therapeutic to mutter these verses to yourself, too – surely a more absorbing, and therefore more effective, technique than counting to ten in an effort to control your temper.

William Blake (1757–1827)

A Poison Tree

I was angry with my friend:
I told my wrath, my wrath did end.
I was angry with my foe:
I told it not, my wrath did grow.

And I watered it in fears,
Night & morning with my tears;
And I sunned it with smiles,
And with soft deceitful wiles.

And it grew both day and night,
Till it bore an apple bright.
And my foe beheld it shine,
And he knew that it was mine,

And into my garden stole,
When the night had veild the pole;
In the morning glad I see
My foe outstretched beneath the tree.

Mary Robinson (1757–1800)

January, 1795

Robinson's howl against the perfidious world is the perfect mental accompaniment to reading a letter of rejection.

Pavement slipp'ry, people sneezing,
Lords in ermine, beggars freezing;
Titled gluttons dainties carving,

Genius in a garret starving.

Lofty mansions, warm and spacious;
Courtiers cringing and voracious;
Misers scarce the wretched heeding;
Gallant soldiers fighting, bleeding.

Wives who laugh at passive spouses;
Theatres, and meeting-houses;
Balls, where simp'ring misses languish;
Hospitals, and groans of anguish.

Arts and sciences bewailing;
Commerce drooping, Credit failing;
Placemen mocking subjects loyal;
Separations, weddings royal.

Authors who can't earn a dinner;
Many a subtle rogue a winner;
Fugitives for shelter seeking;
Misers hoarding, tradesmen breaking.

Taste and talents quite deserted;
All the laws of truth perverted;
Arrogance o'er merit soaring;
Merit silently deploring.

Ladies gambling night and morning;
Fools the works of genius scorning;
Ancient dames for girls mistaken,
Youthful damsels quite forsaken.

Some in luxury delighting;
More in talking than in fighting;
Lovers old, and beaux decrepid;
Lordlings empty and insipid.

Poets, painters, and musicians;
Lawyers, doctors, politicians:
Pamphlets, newspapers, and odes,
Seeking fame, by diff'rent roads.

Gallant Souls with empty purses,
Gen'rals only fit for nurses;
School-boys, smit with martial spirit,
Taking place of vet'ran merit.

Honest men who can't get places;
Knaves who shew unblushing faces;
Ruin hasten'd, peace retarded;
Candour spurn'd, and art rewarded!

Ben Jonson (1572–1637)

To Fool or Knave

*This couplet forms a handy motto to repeat to oneself when faced
with unwanted criticism.*

Thy praise or dispraise is to me alike:
One doth not stroke me, nor the other strike.

Charles Lamb (1775–1834)

Anger

If revelling in your anger is proving overly poisonous, Lamb's poem
will remind you of the danger of luxuriating in it.

Anger in its time and place
May assume a kind of grace.
It must have some reason in it,
And not last beyond a minute.
If to further lengths it go,
It does into malice grow.
'Tis the difference that we see
'Twixt the serpent and the bee.
If the latter you provoke,
It inflicts a hasty stroke,
Puts you to some little pain,
But it never stings again.
Close in tufted bush or brake
Lurks the poison-swellěd snake
Nursing up his cherished wrath;
In the purlieux of his path,
In the cold, or in the warm,
Mean him good, or mean him harm,
Whensoever fate may bring you,
The vile snake will always sting you.

Emily Dickinson (1830–1886)

Part One: Life. LXVIII

Mine enemy is growing old,—
I have at last revenge.
The palate of the hate departs;
If any would avenge,—

Let him be quick, the viand flits,
It is a faded meat.
Anger as soon as fed is dead;
'T is starving makes it fat.

J.M. Synge (1871–1909)

The Curse

Lord, confound this surly sister,
Blight her brow with blotch and blister,
Cramp her larynx, lung, and liver,
In her guts a galling give her.
Let her live to earn her dinners
In Mountjoy with seedy sinners:
Lord, this judgment quickly bring,
And I'm your servant, J. M. Synge.

Ben Jonson (1572–1637)

An Ode to Himself

Where dost thou careless lie
   Buried in ease and sloth?
Knowledge that sleeps doth die;
And this security,
   It is the common moth
That eats on wits and arts, and oft destroys them both.

Are all th' Aonian springs
   Dried up? Lies Thespia waste?
Doth Clarius' harp want strings,
That not a nymph now sings,
   Or droop they as disgraced,
To see their seats and bowers by chattering pies defaced?

If hence thy silence be,
   As 'tis too just a cause,
Let this thought quicken thee:
Minds that are great and free
   Should not on fortune pause;
'Tis crown enough to virtue still, her own applause.

What though the greedy fry
   Be taken with false baits
Of worded balladry,
And think it poesy?
   They die with their conceits,
And only piteous scorn upon their folly waits.

Then take in hand thy lyre,
    Strike in thy proper strain,
  With Japhet's line, aspire
  Sol's chariot for new fire
    To give the world again;
Who aided him will thee, the issue of Jove's brain.

  And since our dainty age
    Cannot endure reproof,
  Make not thyself a page
  To that strumpet the stage,
    But sing high and aloof,
Safe from the wolf's black jaw, and the dull ass's hoof.

Seven

From dappled things to stinking sprats: Nature, in Town and Country

The natural world has inspired many of our greatest poets, and it is wonderful to find a turn of phrase that perfectly conveys the feeling that landscape and creatures impart on the keen observer. Wordsworth composed his poems while roaming his beloved Lake District, and all of the verses that follow would be set beautifully to the rhythm of feet undertaking a country walk or, in the case of Swift's hymn to an urban shower, pounding pavements.

Joyce Kilmer (1886–1918)

Trees

I think that I shall never see
A poem lovely as a tree.

A tree whose hungry mouth is prest
Against the earth's sweet flowing breast;

A tree that looks at God all day,
And lifts her leafy arms to pray;

A tree that may in Summer wear
A nest of robins in her hair;

Upon whose bosom snow has lain;
Who intimately lives with rain.

Poems are made by fools like me,
But only God can make a tree.

Philip Larkin (1922–85)

The Trees

The trees are coming into leaf
Like something almost being said;
The recent buds relax and spread,
Their greenness is a kind of grief.

Is it that they are born again
And we grow old? No, they die too.
Their yearly trick of looking new
Is written down in rings of grain.

Yet still the unresting castles thresh
In fullgrown thickness every May.
Last year is dead, they seem to say,
Begin afresh, afresh, afresh.

William Wordsworth (1770–1850)

The Tables Turned

Wordsworth's poem strikes a chord with anyone who has struggled
to study while witnessing a summer's day from the library window.

Up! up! my Friend, and quit your books;
Or surely you'll grow double:
Up! up! my Friend, and clear your looks;
Why all this toil and trouble?

The sun, above the mountain's head,
A freshening lustre mellow
Through all the long green fields has spread,
His first sweet evening yellow.

Books!, 'tis a dull and endless strife:
Come, hear the woodland linnet,
How sweet his music! on my life,
There's more of wisdom in it.

And hark! how blithe the throstle sings!
He, too, is no mean preacher:
Come forth into the light of things,
Let Nature be your Teacher.

She has a world of ready wealth,
Our minds and hearts to bless—

Spontaneous wisdom breathed by health,
Truth breathed by cheerfulness.

One impulse from a vernal wood
May teach you more of man,
Of moral evil and of good,
Than all the sages can.

Sweet is the lore which Nature brings;
Our meddling intellect
Mis-shapes the beauteous forms of things:—
We murder to dissect.

Enough of Science and of Art;
Close up those barren leaves;
Come forth, and bring with you a heart
That watches and receives.

Robert Burns (1759–96)

Green Grow the Rashes

Green grow the rashes, O;
Green grow the rashes, O;
The sweetest hours that e'er I spend,
Are spent amang the lasses, O!

There's nought but care on ev'ry han',
In ev'ry hour that passes, O:
What signifies the life o' man,
An' 'twere na for the lasses, O.

The warly race may riches chase,
An' riches still may fly them, O;
An' though at last they catch them fast,

Their hearts can ne'er enjoy them, O.

But gie me a canny hour at e'en,
    My arms about my Dearie, O;
An' warly cares, an' warly men,
    May a' gae tapsalteerie, O!

For you sae douce, ye sneer at this,
    Ye're nought but senseless asses, O:
The wisest man the warl' saw,
    He dearly loved the lasses, O.

Auld Nature swears, the lovely Dears
    Her noblest work she classes, O:
Her prentice han' she tried on man,
    An' then she made the lasses, O.

John Keats (1795–1821)

To Autumn

Season of mists and mellow fruitfulness,
    Close bosom-friend of the maturing sun,
Conspiring with him how to load and bless
    With fruit the vines that round the thatch-eves run;
To bend with apples the mossed cottage-trees,
    And fill all fruit with ripeness to the core;
        To swell the gourd, and plump the hazel shells
    With a sweet kernel; to set budding more,
And still more, later flowers for the bees,
Until they think warm days will never cease,
    For Summer has o'er-brimmed their clammy cells.

Who hath not seen thee oft amid thy store?
    Sometimes whoever seeks abroad may find

Thee sitting careless on a granary floor,
    Thy hair soft-lifted by the winnowing wind;
Or on a half-reaped furrow sound asleep,
    Drowsed with the fume of poppies, while thy hook
        Spares the next swath and all its twinèd flowers;
And sometimes like a gleaner thou dost keep
    Steady thy laden head across a brook;
    Or by a cider-press, with patient look,
        Thou watchest the last oozings hours by hours.

Where are the songs of Spring? Ay, where are they?
    Think not of them, thou hast thy music too—
While barrèd clouds bloom the soft-dying day,
    And touch the stubble-plains with rosy hue:
Then in a wailful choir the small gnats mourn
    Among the river sallows, borne aloft
        Or sinking as the light wind lives or dies;
And full-grown lambs loud bleat from hilly bourn;
    Hedge-crickets sing; and now with treble soft
    The red-breast whistles from a garden-croft;
        And gathering swallows twitter in the skies.

William Wordsworth (1770–1850)

I Wandered Lonely as a Cloud

This is probably one of the most commonly memorized poems in the English language, but you will certainly be in the minority if you can recall all the verses.

I wandered lonely as a cloud
That floats on high o'er vales and hills,
When all at once I saw a crowd,
A host, of golden daffodils;
Beside the lake, beneath the trees,
Fluttering and dancing in the breeze.

Continuous as the stars that shine
And twinkle on the milky way,
They stretched in never-ending line
Along the margin of a bay:
Ten thousand saw I at a glance,
Tossing their heads in sprightly dance.

The waves beside them danced; but they
Out-did the sparkling waves in glee:
A poet could not but be gay,
In such a jocund company:
I gazed—and gazed—but little thought
What wealth the show to me had brought:

For oft, when on my couch I lie
In vacant or in pensive mood,
They flash upon that inward eye
Which is the bliss of solitude;
And then my heart with pleasure fills,
And dances with the daffodils.

Gerard Manley Hopkins (1844–99)

Pied Beauty

Hopkins's works are not easy to learn because he loved to write with a flickering (so-called sprung) rhythm. Once mastered, these pauses enable the speaker to relish each of his gorgeous descriptive phrases.

Glory be to God for dappled things—
    For skies of couple-colour as a brinded cow;
     For rose-moles all in stipple upon trout that swim;
Fresh-firecoal chestnut-falls; finches' wings;
    Landscape plotted and pieced—fold, fallow, and plough;
     And áll trádes, their gear and tackle and trim.

All things counter, original, spare, strange;
    Whatever is fickle, freckled (who knows how?)
     With swift, slow; sweet, sour; adazzle, dim;
He fathers-forth whose beauty is past change:
                Praise him.

As kingfishers catch fire, dragonflies draw flame;
    As tumbled over rim in roundy wells
    Stones ring; like each tucked string tells, each hung bell's
Bow swung finds tongue to fling out broad its name;
Each mortal thing does one thing and the same:
    Deals out that being indoors each one dwells;
    Selves—goes its self; *myself* it speaks and spells,
Crying *What I do is me: for that I came.*

Í say more: the just man justices;
    Keeps gráce: thát keeps all his goings graces;
Acts in God's eye what in God's eye he is—

Christ. For Christ plays in ten thousand places,
Lovely in limbs, and lovely in eyes not his
　To the Father through the features of men's faces.

Jonathan Swift (1667–1745)

A Description of a City Shower

　Careful Observers may fortell the hour
(By sure prognostics) when to dread a shower:
While rain depends, the pensive cat gives o'er
Her frolics, and pursues her tail no more.
Returning home at night, you'll find the sink
Strike your offended sense with double stink.
If you be wise, then go not far to dine;
You'll spend in coach hire more than save in wine.
A coming shower your shooting corns presage,
Old achès throb, your hollow tooth will rage.
Sauntering in coffeehouse is Dulman seen;
He damns the climate and complains of spleen.
　Meanwhile the South, rising with dabbled wings,
A sable cloud athwart the welkin flings,
That swilled more liquor than it could contain,
And, like a drunkard, gives it up again.
Brisk Susan whips her linen from the rope,
While the first drizzling shower is born aslope:
Such is that sprinkling which some careless quean
Flirts on you from her mop, but not so clean:
You fly, invoke the gods; then turning, stop
To rail; she singing, still whirls on her mop.
Not yet the dust had shunned the unequal strife,
But, aided by the wind, fought still for life,

And wafted with its foe by violent gust,
'Twas doubtful which was rain, and which was dust.
Ah! where must needy poet seek for aid,
When dust and rain at once his coat invade?
Sole coat, where dust cemented by the rain
Erects the nap, and leaves a mingled stain.

    Now in contiguous drops the flood comes down,
Threatening with deluge this devoted town.
To shops in crowds the daggled females fly,
Pretend to cheapen goods, but nothing buy.
The Templar spruce, while every spout's abroach,
Stays till 'tis fair, yet seems to call a coach.
The tucked-up sempstress walks with hasty strides,
While streams run down her oiled umbrella's sides.
Here various kinds, by various fortunes led,
Commence acquaintance underneath a shed.
Triumphant Tories and desponding Whigs
Forget their feuds, and join to save their wigs.
Boxed in a chair the beau impatient sits,
While spouts run clattering o'er the roof by fits,
And ever and anon with frightful din
The leather sounds; he trembles from within.
So when Troy chairmen bore the wooden steed,
Pregnant with Greeks impatient to be freed
(Those bully Greeks, who, as the moderns do,
Instead of paying chairmen, run them through),
Laocoön struck the outside with his spear,
And each imprisoned hero quaked for fear.

    Now from all parts the swelling kennels flow,
And bear their trophies with them as they go:
Filth of all hues and odors seem to tell
What street they sailed from, by their sight and smell.

They, as each torrent drives with rapid force,
From Smithfield or St. Pulchre's shape their course,
And in huge confluence joined at Snow Hill ridge,
Fall from the conduit prone to Holborn Bridge.
Sweepings from butchers' stalls, dung, guts, and blood,
Drowned puppies, stinking sprats, all drenched in mud,
Dead cats, and turnips tops, come tumbling down the flood.

William Wordsworth (1770–1850)

My Heart Leaps Up When I Behold

My heart leaps up when I behold
    A rainbow in the sky:
So was it when my life began;
So is it now I am a man;
So be it when I shall grow old,
    Or let me die!
The Child is father of the Man;
And I could wish my days to be
Bound each to each by natural piety.

William Shakespeare (1564–1616)

Ariel's songs from *The Tempest*

Where the bee sucks, there suck I:
In a cowslip's bell I lie;
There I couch when owls do cry.
On the bat's back I do fly
After summer merrily.
Merrily, merrily shall I live now

Under the blossom that hangs on the bough.

. . .

Come unto these yellow sands,
    And then take hands:
Court'sied when you have, and kiss'd—
    The wild waves whist,—
Foot it featly here and there;
And, sweet sprites, the burthen bear.
        Hark, hark!
            Bow wow,
        The watch-dogs bark:
            Bow wow,
        Hark, hark! I hear
    The strain of strutting chanticleer
    Cry, Cock-a-diddle-dow!

. . .

Full fathom five thy father lies;
    Of his bones are coral made;
Those are pearls that were his eyes:
    Nothing of him that doth fade,
But doth suffer a sea-change
Into something rich and strange.
Sea-nymphs hourly ring his knell:
            Ding-dong.
    Hark! now I hear them—
            Ding-dong, bell!

Thomas Hood (1799–1845)

No!

No sun–no moon!
No morn–no noon!
No dawn–no dusk–no proper time of day–
No sky–no earthly view–
No distance looking blue–
No road–no street–no 't'other side this way'–
No end to any Row–
No indications where the Crescents go–
No top to any steeple–
No recognitions of familiar people–
No courtesies for showing 'em–
No knowing 'em!
No travelling at all–no locomotion–
No inkling of the way–no notion–
'No go' by land or ocean–
No mail–no post–
No news from any foreign coast–
No Park, no Ring, no afternoon gentility–
No company–no nobility–
No warmth, no cheerfulness, no healthful ease,
No comfortable feel in any member–
No shade, no shine, no butterflies, no bees,
No fruits, no flowers, no leaves, no birds–
November!

Robert Louis Stevenson (1850–94)

Bed in Summer

*It is difficult to think of another poem that so encapsulates a
child's-eye view of the strange and illogical tyranny of grown-up
people's rules.*

In winter I get up at night
And dress by yellow candle-light.
In summer quite the other way,
I have to go to bed by day.

I have to go to bed and see
The birds still hopping on the tree,
Or hear the grown-up people's feet
Still going past me in the street.

And does it not seem hard to you,
When all the sky is clear and blue,
And I should like so much to play,
To have to go to bed by day?

John Dryden (1631–1700)

Of Many Worlds in This World

Modern science has inured us to the wonders of the microscope, but Dryden's short poem rekindles a true sense of wonder.

Just like as in a nest of boxes round,
Degrees of sizes in each box are found:
So, in this world, may many others be
Thinner and less, and less still by degree:
Although they are not subject to our sense,
A world may be no bigger than two-pence.
Nature is curious, and such works may shape,
Which our dull senses easily escape:
For creatures, small as atoms, may be there,
If every one a creature's figure bear.
If atoms four, a world can make, then see
What several worlds might in an ear-ring be:
For, millions of these atoms may be in
The head of one small, little, single pin.
And if thus small, then ladies may well wear
A world of worlds, as pendents in each ear.

'It will take me about a month to learn ... but in
the end I'll be the possessor of a nice big piece of
poetical real estate, one that I will always be able
to revisit and roam about in.'

Jim Holt, *New York Times*, 2 April 2009

Eight

Four-footed, tiptoe: Beasts

I cannot be the only person who has been caught serenading a family pet with poetry. (It was Eliot's 'Jellicle Cats' and my feline audience was deeply unimpressed.) Wild, domestic and mythological beasts have all inspired memorable poems, and these are often the verses we learn as children. Like nursery rhymes, the poems we commit to memory in our earliest years seem to stay with us all our lives. The parents of children who manage to spot verses missed from their favourite poetry book (usually in a vain attempt by the adult to hasten bedtime) will confirm the poetry-learning capabilities of even the very young.

T.S. Eliot (1888–1965)

The Naming of Cats

Eliot's sentiment rings especially true in the vet's waiting room, when someone has to rise when an embarrassing pet's name is called. Take this poem to heart, then, and give your pet a name you'll be proud to shout across the park.

The Naming of Cats is a difficult matter,
It isn't just one of your holiday games;
You may think at first I'm as mad as a hatter
When I tell you, a cat must have THREE DIFFERENT
    NAMES.
First of all, there's the name that the family use daily,
Such as Peter, Augustus, Alonzo or James,
Such as Victor or Jonathan, George or Bill Bailey –
All of them sensible everyday names.
There are fancier names if you think they sound sweeter,
Some for the gentlemen, some for the dames:
Such as Plato, Admetus, Electra, Demeter –
But all of them sensible everyday names.
But I tell you, a cat needs a name that's particular,
A name that's peculiar, and more dignified,
Else how can he keep up his tail perpendicular,
Or spread out his whiskers, or cherish his pride?
Of names of this kind, I can give you a quorum,
Such as Munkustrap, Quaxo, or Coricopat,
Such as Bombalurina, or else Jellylorum –
Names that never belong to more than one cat.
But above and beyond there's still one name left over,
And that is the name that you never will guess;
The name that no human research can discover –

But THE CAT HIMSELF KNOWS, and will never confess.
When you notice a cat in profound meditation,
The reason, I tell you, is always the same:
His mind is engaged in a rapt contemplation
Of the thought, of the thought, of the thought of his name:
His ineffable effable
Effanineffable
Deep and inscrutable singular Name.

Thomas Hardy (1840–1928)

The Fallow Deer at the Lonely House

One without looks in tonight
Through the curtain-chink
From the sheet of glistening white;
One without looks in tonight
As we sit and think
By the fender-brink.

We do not discern those eyes
Watching in the snow;
Lit by lamps of rosy dyes
We do not discern those eyes
Wandering, aglow
Four-footed, tiptoe.

Lewis Carroll (1832–98)

Jabberwocky

It is surprising how many people do know 'Jabberwocky' by heart, as memorising nonsense poems is fraught with difficulties – you may be making up your own words, instead of Carroll's.

'Twas brillig, and the slithy toves
    Did gyre and gimble in the wabe:
All mimsy were the borogoves,
    And the mome raths outgrabe.

'Beware the Jabberwock, my son!
    The jaws that bite, the claws that catch!
Beware the Jubjub bird, and shun
    The frumious Bandersnatch!'

He took his vorpal sword in hand:
    Long time the manxome foe he sought—
So rested he by the Tumtum tree,
    And stood awhile in thought.

And, as in uffish thought he stood,
    The Jabberwock, with eyes of flame,
Came whiffling through the tulgey wood,
    And burbled as it came!

Gerard Manley Hopkins (1844–99)

The Windhover

To Christ Our Lord

I caught this morning morning's minion, king-
    dom of daylight's dauphin, dapple-dawn-drawn Falcon, in
      his riding
    Of the rolling level underneath him steady air, and striding
High there, how he rung upon the rein of a wimpling wing
In his ecstasy! then off, off forth on swing,
    As a skate's heel sweeps smooth on a bow-bend: the hurl and
      gliding
    Rebuffed the big wind. My heart in hiding
Stirred for a bird,—the achieve of, the mastery of the thing!
Brute beauty and valour and act, oh, air, pride, plume, here
    Buckle! AND the fire that breaks from thee then, a billion
Times told lovelier, more dangerous, O my chevalier!

    No wonder of it: shéer plód makes plough down sillion
Shine, and blue-bleak embers, ah my dear,
    Fall, gall themselves, and gash gold-vermilion.

Edward Lear (1812–88)

The Owl and the Pussy-Cat

The dreamy sing-song rhythm of Lear's most famous poem gives it the pleasing quality of a lullaby, so it isn't surprising that many of us learnt it as children and can recall it still.

The Owl and the Pussy-cat went to sea
In a beautiful pea-green boat,
They took some honey, and plenty of money,
Wrapped up in a five-pound note.
The Owl looked up to the stars above,
And sang to a small guitar,
'O lovely Pussy! O Pussy, my love,
What a beautiful Pussy you are,
You are,
You are!
What a beautiful Pussy you are.'

Pussy said to the Owl, 'You elegant fowl!
How charmingly sweet you sing!
O let us be married! too long we have tarried:
But what shall we do for a ring?'
They sailed away, for a year and a day,
To the land where the Bong-tree grows,
And there in a wood a Piggy-wig stood,
With a ring at the end of his nose,
His nose,
His nose,
With a ring at the end of his nose.

'Dear Pig, are you willing to sell for one shilling
Your ring?' Said the Piggy, 'I will.'

So they took it away, and were married next day
By the Turkey who lives on the hill.
They dinèd on mince, and slices of quince,
Which they ate with a runcible spoon;
And hand in hand, on the edge of the sand,
They danced by the light of the moon,
The moon,
The moon,
They danced by the light of the moon.

Thomas Hardy (1840–1928)

The Darkling Thrush

I leant upon a coppice gate
    When Frost was spectre-gray,
And Winter's dregs made desolate
    The weakening eye of day.
The tangled bine-stems scored the sky
    Like strings of broken lyres,
And all mankind that haunted nigh
    Had sought their household fires.

The land's sharp features seemed to be
    The Century's corpse outleant,
His crypt the cloudy canopy,
    The wind his death-lament.
The ancient pulse of germ and birth
    Was shrunken hard and dry,
And every spirit upon earth
    Seemed fervourless as I.

At once a voice arose among

The bleak twigs overhead
In a full-hearted evensong
   Of joy illimited;
An aged thrush, frail, gaunt and small,
   In blast-beruffled plume,
Had chosen thus to fling his soul
   Upon the growing gloom.

So little cause for carolings
   Of such ecstatic sound
Was written on terrestrial things
   Afar or nigh around,
That I could think there trembled through
   His happy good-night air
Some blessed Hope, whereof he knew
   And I was unaware.

Lewis Carroll (1832–98)

A Whiting and A Snail

This delightful verse details the intricacies of the Lobster Quadrille. Once you know it, it's difficult not to find yourself beginning it whenever you find yourself behind a slowcoach, although good manners would dictate that you recite it only in your head.

'Will you walk a little faster?' said a whiting to a snail.
'There's a porpoise close behind us, and he's treading on my tail.
See how eagerly the lobsters and the turtles all advance!
They are waiting on the shingle – will you come and join the
   dance?
Will you, won't you, will you, won't you, will you join the
   dance?

Will you, won't you, will you, won't you, won't you join the
dance?

'You can really have no notion how delightful it will be
When they take us up and throw us, with the lobsters, out to
sea!'
But the snail replied 'Too far, too far!' and gave a look askance –
Said he thanked the whiting kindly, but he would not join the
dance.
Would not, could not, would not, could not, would not join the
dance.
Would not, could not, would not, could not, could not join the
dance.

'What matters it how far we go?' his scaly friend replied.
'There is another shore, you know, upon the other side.
The further off from England the nearer is to France –
Then turn not pale, beloved snail, but come and join the dance.
Will you, won't you, will you, won't you, will you join the
dance?
Will you, won't you, will you, won't you, won't you join the
dance?'

Alfred, Lord Tennyson (1809–92)

The Kraken

> Below the thunders of the upper deep;
> Far, far beneath in the abysmal sea,
> His ancient, dreamless, uninvaded sleep
> The Kraken sleepeth: faintest sunlights flee
> About his shadowy sides: above him swell
> Huge sponges of millennial growth and height;

And far away into the sickly light,
From many a wondrous grot and secret cell
Unnumbered and enormous polypi
Winnow with giant fins the slumbering green.
There hath he lain for ages and will lie
Battening upon huge seaworms in his sleep,
Until the latter fire shall heat the deep;
Then once by men and angels to be seen,
In roaring he shall rise and on the surface die.

T.S. Eliot (1888–1965)

Skimbleshanks: The Railway Cat

There's a whisper down the line at 11:39
When the Night Mail's ready to depart,
Saying 'Skimble where is Skimble has he gone to hunt the thimble?
We must find him or the train can't start.'
All the guards and all the porters and the stationmaster's daughters
They are searching high and low,
Saying 'Skimble where is Skimble for unless he's very nimble
Then the Night Mail just can't go.'
At 11:42 then the signal's nearly due
And the passengers are frantic to a man—
Then Skimble will appear and he'll saunter to the rear:
He's been busy in the luggage van!
    He gives one flash of his glass-green eyes
        And the signal goes 'All Clear!'
    And we're off at last for the northern part
        Of the Northern Hemisphere!

You may say that by and large it is Skimble who's in charge
Of the Sleeping Car Express.
From the driver and the guards to the bagmen playing cards
He will supervise them all, more or less.
Down the corridor he paces and examines all the faces
Of the travellers in the First and in the Third;
He establishes control by a regular patrol
And he'd know at once if anything occurred.
He will watch you without winking and he sees what you are
thinking
And it's certain that he doesn't approve
Of hilarity and riot, so the folk are very quiet
When Skimble is about and on the move.
        You can play no pranks with Skimbleshanks!
                He's a Cat that cannot be ignored;
        So nothing goes wrong on the Northern Mail
                When Skimbleshanks is aboard.

Oh it's very pleasant when you have found your little den
With your name written up on the door.
And the berth is very neat with a newly folded sheet
And there's not a speck of dust on the floor.
There is every sort of light — you can make it dark or bright;
There's a handle that you turn to make a breeze.
There's a funny little basin you're supposed to wash your face in
And a crank to shut the window if you sneeze.
Then the guard looks in politely and will ask you very brightly
'Do you like your morning tea weak or strong?'
But Skimble's just behind him and was ready to remind him,
For Skimble won't let anything go wrong.
        And when you creep into your cosy berth
                And pull up the counterpane,
        You ought to reflect that it's very nice

To know that you won't be bothered by mice—
You can leave all that to the Railway Cat,
    The Cat of the Railway Train!

In the watches of the night he is always fresh and bright;
Every now and then he has a cup of tea
With perhaps a drop of Scotch while he's keeping on the watch,
Only stopping here and there to catch a flea.
You were fast asleep at Crewe and so you never knew
That he was walking up and down the station;
You were sleeping all the while he was busy at Carlisle,
Where he greets the stationmaster with elation.
But you saw him at Dumfries, where he speaks to the police
If there's anything they ought to know about:
When you get to Gallowgate there you do not have to wait—
For Skimbleshanks will help you to get out!
    He gives you a wave of his long brown tail
        Which says: 'I'll see you again!
    You'll meet without fail on the Midnight Mail
        The Cat of the Railway Train.'

Nine

Stopping, and staring: Reflection

It is not often, in today's busy world, that we can enjoy the luxury of time to reflect quietly. These are poems for a snatched few minutes; words to relax and rejuvenate. They are the poetic equivalent of a hot bath or cup of tea, and, once learnt, are easy to recall during a hectic day.

W.H. Davies (1871–1940)

Leisure

Here is a hymn to tranquillity, with words to reassure us that a moment of quiet idleness is not only excusable but positively necessary from time to time.

What is this life if, full of care,
We have no time to stand and stare?—

No time to stand beneath the boughs,
And stare as long as sheep and cows:

No time to see, when woods we pass,
Where squirrels hide their nuts in grass:

No time to see, in broad daylight,
Streams full of stars, like skies at night:

No time to turn at Beauty's glance,
And watch her feet, how they can dance:

No time to wait till her mouth can
Enrich that smile her eyes began?

A poor life this if, full of care,
We have no time to stand and stare.

William Wordsworth (1770–1850)

A Slumber Did My Spirit Seal

A slumber did my spirit seal;
    I had no human fears:
She seem'd a thing that could not feel

The touch of earthly years.

No motion has she now, no force;
    She neither hears nor sees;
Roll'd round in earth's diurnal course,
    With rocks, and stones, and trees.

Alexander Pope (1688–1744)

Ode on Solitude

Happy the man, whose wish and care
A few paternal acres bound,
Content to breathe his native air,
    In his own ground.

Whose herds with milk, whose fields with bread,
Whose flocks supply him with attire,
Whose trees in summer yield him shade,
    In winter fire.

Blest! who can unconcern'dly find
Hours, days, and years slide soft away,
In health of body, peace of mind,
    Quiet by day,

Sound sleep by night; study and ease
Together mix'd; sweet recreation,
And innocence, which most does please,
    With meditation.

Thus let me live, unseen, unknown;
Thus unlamented let me die;
Steal from the world, and not a stone
    Tell where I lie.

Robert Frost (1874–1963)

Stopping by Woods on a Snowy Evening

Whose woods these are I think I know.
His house is in the village, though;
He will not see me stopping here
To watch his woods fill up with snow.

My little horse must think it queer
To stop without a farmhouse near
Between the woods and frozen lake
The darkest evening of the year.

He gives his harness bells a shake
To ask if there is some mistake.
The only other sound's the sweep
Of easy wind and downy flake.

The woods are lovely, dark and deep,
But I have promises to keep,
And miles to go before I sleep,
And miles to go before I sleep.

Coventry Patmore (1823–96)

Magna est Veritas

Here, in this little Bay,
Full of tumultuous life and great repose,
Where, twice a day,
The purposeless, glad ocean comes and goes,
Under high cliffs, and far from the huge town,
I sit me down.
For want of me the world's course will not fail:
When all its work is done, the lie shall rot;
The truth is great, and shall prevail,
When none cares whether it prevail or not.

Thomas Hardy (1840–1928)

In Time of 'The Breaking of Nations'

Only a man harrowing clods
In a slow silent walk
With an old horse that stumbles and nods
Half asleep as they stalk.

Only thin smoke without flame
From the heaps of couch-grass;
Yet this will go onward the same
Though Dynasties pass.

Yonder a maid and her wight
Come whispering by:
War's annals will cloud into night
Ere their story die.

Emily Dickinson (1830–86)

935 'As imperceptibly as Grief'

As imperceptibly as Grief
The Summer lapsed away -
Too imperceptible at last
To seem like Perfidy -
A Quietness distilled
As Twilight long begun,
Or Nature spending with herself
Sequestered Afternoon -
The Dusk drew earlier in -
The Morning foreign shone -
A courteous, yet harrowing Grace,
As Guest, that would be gone -
And thus, without a Wing
Or service of a Keel
Our Summer made her light escape
Into the Beautiful -

W.B. Yeats (1865–1939)

The Lake Isle of Innisfree

I will arise and go now, and go to Innisfree,
And a small cabin build there, of clay and wattles made:
Nine bean-rows will I have there, a hive for the honey-bee,
And live alone in the bee-loud glade.

And I shall have some peace there,
    for peace comes dropping slow,
Dropping from the veils of the morning
    to where the cricket sings;
There midnight's all a glimmer, and noon a purple glow,
And evening full of the linnet's wings.

I will arise and go now, for always night and day
I hear lake water lapping with low sounds by the shore;
While I stand on the roadway, or on the pavements gray,
I hear it in the deep heart's core.

'Poetry is the breath and finer spirit of all
knowledge.'

William Wordsworth

Ten

Striving against swaddling bands: Family

A celebration of the ties that bind, the verses in this chapter underline the universal nature of the familial experience.

William Blake (1757–1827)

Infant Sorrow

My mother groand! my father wept,
Into the dangerous world I leapt;
Helpless, naked, piping loud;
Like a fiend hid in a cloud.

Struggling in my fathers hands,
Striving against my swaddling bands:
Bound and weary, I thought best
To sulk upon my mothers breast.

Wilfrid Wilson Gibson (1878–1962)

Air Raid

*This poem looks at war from an unusual and moving angle – that
of parents whose anxious early nights with their young child are
lived against a backdrop of terror.*

Night shatters in mid-heaven – the bark of guns,
The roar of planes, the crash of bombs, and all
The unshackled skyey pandemonium stuns
The senses to indifference, when a fall
Of masonry near by startles awake,
Tingling, wide-eyed, prick-eared, with bristling hair,
Each sense within the body crouched aware
Like some sore-hunted creature in the brake.

Yet side by side we lie in the little room,
Just touching hands, with eyes and ears that strain
Keenly, yet dream-bewildered, through tense gloom,

Listening in helpless stupor of insane
Drugged nightmare panic fantastically wild,
To the quiet breathing of our sleeping child.

Philip Larkin (1922–85)

This Be the Verse

*Larkin's poem is particularly well known – who doesn't enjoy a
rude word? – and frequently parodied or paraphrased.*

They fuck you up, your mum and dad.
They may not mean to, but they do.
They fill you with the faults they had
And add some extra, just for you.

But they were fucked up in their turn
By fools in old-style hats and coats,
Who half the time were soppy-stern
And half at one another's throats.

Man hands on misery to man.
It deepens like a coastal shelf.
Get out as early as you can,
And don't have any kids yourself.

D.H. Lawrence (1885–1930)

Piano

Softly, in the dusk, a woman is singing to me;
Taking me back down the vista of years, till I see
A child sitting under the piano, in the boom of the tingling strings
And pressing the small, poised feet of a mother who smiles as she sings.

In spite of myself, the insidious mastery of song
Betrays me back, till the heart of me weeps to belong
To the old Sunday evenings at home, with winter outside
And hymns in the cosy parlour, the tinkling piano our guide.

So now it is vain for the singer to burst into clamour
With the great black piano appassionato. The glamour
Of childish days is upon me, my manhood is cast
Down in the flood of remembrance, I weep like a child for the past.

A.A. Milne (1882–1956)

Disobedience

James James
Morrison Morrison
Weatherby George Dupree
Took great
Care of his Mother,
Though he was only three.
James James
Said to his Mother,
"Mother," he said, said he;
"You must never go down to the end of the town,
if you don't go down with me."

James James
Morrison's Mother
Put on a golden gown,
James James
Morrison's Mother
Drove to the end of the town.
James James
Morrison's Mother
Said to herself, said she:
"I can get right down to the end of the town and be
back in time for tea."

King John
Put up a notice,
"LOST or STOLEN or STRAYED!
JAMES JAMES
MORRISON'S MOTHER
SEEMS TO HAVE BEEN MISLAID.
LAST SEEN
WANDERING VAGUELY:
QUITE OF HER OWN ACCORD,
SHE TRIED TO GET DOWN TO THE END OF THE
TOWN—**FORTY SHILLINGS REWARD!**"

James James
Morrison Morrison
(Commonly known as Jim)   Told his
Other relations
Not to go blaming *him*.
James James
Said to his Mother,
"Mother," he said, said he:
"You must *never* go down to the end of the town

without consulting me."

    James James
    Morrison's mother
    Hasn't been heard of since.
    King John
    Said he was sorry,
    So did the Queen and Prince.
    King John
    (Somebody told me)
    Said to a man he knew:
"If people go down to the end of the town, well,
    what can *anyone* do?"

(*Now then, very softly*)
    J. J.
    M. M.
    W. G. Du P.
    Took great
    C/o his M*****
    Though he was only 3.
    J. J.
    Said to his M*****
    "M*****," he said, said he:
"You-must-never-go-down-to-the-end-of-the-town-
if-you-don't-go-down-with-ME!"

Frances Cornford (1886–1960)

Childhood

I used to think that grown-up people chose
To have stiff backs and wrinkles round their nose,
And veins like small fat snakes on either hand,
On purpose to be grand.
Till through the banister I watched one day
My great-aunt Etty's friend who was going away,
And how her onyx beads had come unstrung.
I saw her grope to find them as they rolled;
And then I knew that she was helplessly old,
As I was helplessly young.

Lewis Carroll (1832–98)

Speak Roughly

Speak roughly to your little boy,
And beat him when he sneezes:
He only does it to annoy,
Because he knows it teases.

I speak severely to my boy,
And beat him when he sneezes:
For he can thoroughly enjoy
The pepper when he pleases.

Thomas Gray (1716–71)

Elegy Written in a Country Church Yard [extract]

The Curfew tolls the knell of parting day,
The lowing herd wind slowly o'er the lea,
The plowman homeward plods his weary way,
And leaves the world to darkness and to me.

Now fades the glimmering landscape on the sight,
And all the air a solemn stillness holds,
Save where the beetle wheels his droning flight,
And drowsy tinklings lull the distant folds;

Save that from yonder ivy-mantled tow'r
The moping owl does to the moon complain
Of such, as wand'ring near her secret bow'r,
Molest her ancient solitary reign.

Beneath those rugged elms, that yew tree's shade,
Where heaves the turf in many a mould'ring heap,
Each in his narrow cell forever laid,
The rude Forefathers of the hamlet sleep.

The breezy call of incense-breathing Morn,
The swallow twitt'ring from the straw-built shed,
The cock's shrill clarion, or the echoing horn,
No more shall rouse them from their lowly bed.

For them no more the blazing hearth shall burn,
Or busy housewife ply her evening care:
No children run to lisp their sire's return,
Or climb his knees the envied kiss to share.

Oft did the harvest to their sickle yield,
Their furrow oft the stubborn glebe has broke;

How jocund did they drive their team afield!
How bow'd the woods beneath their sturdy stroke!

Let not Ambition mock their useful toil,
Their homely joys, and destiny obscure;
Nor Grandeur hear with a disdainful smile
The short and simple annals of the poor.

The boast of heraldry, the pomp of pow'r,
And all that beauty, all that wealth e'er gave,
Awaits alike th' inevitable hour.
The paths of glory lead but to the grave.

'I was ten and the poem was written by a thirty-year-old so obviously I didn't understand it. But you learn it off by heart and then, later in life, those words come back to you. You realise the value of poetry.'

John Cooper Clarke,
East Anglian Daily Times, 7 October 2012

Eleven

When you are old and grey: Ageing Gracefully and Disgracefully

While poets often write of glamorous youthful passions and pursuits, they have not neglected to put their feelings about the other end of life into verse. From peaceful words urging acceptance and the enjoyment of a contented dotage to Jenny Joseph's fabulously rebellious 'Warning', here is a collection of poems about advancing in age however you choose to do it.

Thomas Hardy (1840–1928)

Afterwards

When the Present has latched its postern behind my tremulous stay,
    And the May month flaps its glad green leaves like wings,
Delicate-filmed as new-spun silk, will the neighbours say,
    'He was a man who used to notice such things'?

If it be in the dusk when, like an eyelid's soundless blink,
    The dewfall-hawk comes crossing the shades to alight
Upon the wind-warped upland thorn, a gazer may think,
    'To him this must have been a familiar sight'.

If I pass during some nocturnal blackness, mothy and warm,
    When the hedgehog travels furtively over the lawn,
One may say, 'He strove that such innocent creatures should come to
    no harm,
        But he could do little for them; and now he is gone'.

If, when hearing that I have been stilled at last, they stand at the door,
    Watching the full-starred heavens that winter sees,
Will this thought rise on those who will meet my face no more,
    'He was one who had an eye for such mysteries'?

And will any say when my bell of quittance is heard in the gloom,
    And a crossing breeze cuts a pause in its outrollings,
Till they swell again, as they were a new bell's boom,
    'He hears it not now, but used to notice such things'?

William Savage Landor (1775–1864)

To Age

Welcome, old friend! These many years
Have we liv'd door by door:
The Fates have laid aside their shears
Perhaps for some few more.

I was indocile at an age
When better boys were taught,
But thou at length hast made me sage,
If I am sage in aught.

Little I know from other men,
Too little they from me,
But thou hast pointed well the pen
That writes these lines to thee.

Thanks for expelling Fear and Hope,
One vile, the other vain;
One's scourge, the other's telescope,
I shall not see again:

Rather what lies before my feet
My notice shall engage.
He who hath brav'd Youth's dizzy heat
Dreads not the frost of Age.

W.B. Yeats (1865–1939)

When You Are Old

When you are old and grey and full of sleep,
And nodding by the fire, take down this book,
And slowly read, and dream of the soft look
Your eyes had once, and of their shadows deep;

How many loved your moments of glad grace,
And loved your beauty with love false or true,
But one man loved the pilgrim soul in you,
And loved the sorrows of your changing face;

And bending down beside the glowing bars,
Murmur, a little sadly, how Love fled
And paced upon the mountains overhead
And hid his face amid a crowd of stars.

Jenny Joseph (1932–)

Warning

When I am an old woman I shall wear purple
With a red hat which doesn't go, and doesn't suit me.
And I shall spend my pension on brandy and summer gloves
And satin sandals, and say we've no money for butter.
I shall sit down on the pavement when I'm tired
And gobble up samples in shops and press alarm bells
And run my stick along the public railings
And make up for the sobriety of my youth.
I shall go out in my slippers in the rain
And pick the flowers in other people's gardens
And learn to spit.

You can wear terrible shirts and grow more fat
And eat three pounds of sausages at a go
Or only eat bread and pickle for a week
And hoard pens and pencils and beermats and things in boxes.

But now we must have clothes that keep us dry
And pay our rent and not swear in the street
And set a good example for the children.
We must have friends to dinner and read the papers.

But maybe I ought to practise a little now?
So people who know me are not too shocked and surprised
When suddenly I am old, and start to wear purple.

'Even busy lives contain poetry-sized moments.'

Laura Barber, *Poetry by Heart*

Twelve

Into the silent land: Death

Poets rarely shy away from addressing the final mystery of death. Their words have resonated through the ages because, although none of us can look behind that curtain, they express their thoughts on death better than we ever could our own. These are poems both triumphant and gentle, and which generations have reached out to for comfort in times of loss.

Rupert Brooke (1887–1915)

The Soldier

If I should die, think only this of me:
That there's some corner of a foreign field
That is forever England. There shall be
In that rich earth a richer dust concealed;
A dust whom England bore, shaped, made aware,
Gave, once, her flowers to love, her ways to roam,
A body of England's, breathing English air,
Washed by the rivers, blest by suns of home.

And think, this heart, all evil shed away,
A pulse in the eternal mind, no less
Gives somewhere back the thoughts by England given,
Her sights and sounds; dreams happy as her day;
And laughter, learnt of friends; and gentleness,
In hearts at peace, under an English heaven.

Edward Thomas (1878–1917)

Lights Out

I have come to the borders of sleep,
The unfathomable deep
Forest where all must lose
Their way, however straight,
Or winding, soon or late;
They cannot choose.

Many a road and track
That, since the dawn's first crack,
Up to the forest brink,

Deceived the travellers,
Suddenly now blurs,
And in they sink.

Here love ends,
Despair, ambition ends;
All pleasure and all trouble;
Although most sweet or bitter,
Here ends in sleep that is sweeter
Than tasks most noble.

There is not any book
Or face of dearest look
That I would not turn from now
To go into the unknown
I must enter, and leave, alone,
I know not how.

The tall forest towers;
Its cloudy foliage lowers
Ahead, shelf above shelf;
Its silence I hear and obey
That I may lose my way
And myself.

Alexander Pope (1688–1744)

The Dying Christian to his Soul

Vital spark of heav'nly flame!
Quit, O quit this mortal frame:
Trembling, hoping, ling'ring, flying,
O the pain, the bliss of dying!
Cease, fond Nature, cease thy strife,

And let me languish into life.

Hark! they whisper; angels say,
Sister Spirit, come away!
What is this absorbs me quite?
Steals my senses, shuts my sight,
Drowns my spirits, draws my breath?
Tell me, my soul, can this be death?

The world recedes; it disappears!
Heav'n opens on my eyes! my ears
With sounds seraphic ring!
Lend, lend your wings! I mount! I fly!
O Grave! where is thy victory?
O Death! where is thy sting?

W.H. Auden (1907–73)

Funeral Blues

*This bleakly beautiful poem is simple to learn, but deeply affecting.
Its everyday imagery evokes a striking portrait of grief.*

Stop all the clocks, cut off the telephone,
Prevent the dog from barking with a juicy bone,
Silence the pianos and with muffled drum
Bring out the coffin, let the mourners come.

Let aeroplanes circle moaning overhead
Scribbling on the sky the message He is Dead,
Put crêpe bows round the white necks of the public doves,
Let the traffic policemen wear black cotton gloves.

He was my North, my South, my East and West,
My working week and my Sunday rest,

My noon, my midnight, my talk, my song,
I thought that love would last for ever: I was wrong.

The stars are not wanted now: put out every one;
Pack up the moon and dismantle the sun;
Pour away the ocean and sweep up the wood;
For nothing now can ever come to any good.

Christina Rossetti (1830–94)

Remember Me

Remember me when I am gone away,
Gone far away into the silent land;
When you can no more hold me by the hand,
Nor I half turn to go, yet turning stay.
Remember me when no more day by day
You tell me of our future that you planned:
Only remember me; you understand
It will be late to counsel then or pray.
Yet if you should forget me for a while
And afterwards remember, do not grieve:
For if the darkness and corruption leave
A vestige of the thoughts that once I had,
Better by far you should forget and smile
Than that you should remember and be sad.

Edgar Allen Poe (1809–49)

Annabel Lee

It was many and many a year ago,
In a kingdom by the sea,
That a maiden there lived whom you may know
By the name of Annabel Lee;
And this maiden she lived with no other thought
Than to love and be loved by me.

She was a child and I was a child,
In this kingdom by the sea,
But we loved with a love that was more than love –
I and my Annabel Lee –
With a love that the wingèd seraphs of Heaven
Coveted her and me.

And this was the reason that, long ago,
In this kingdom by the sea,
A wind blew out of a cloud by night,
Chilling my beautiful Annabel Lee;
So that her highborn kinsmen came
And bore her away from me,
To shut her up in a sepulchre
In this kingdom by the sea.

The angels, not half so happy in Heaven,
Went envying her and me:
Yes! that was the reason (as all men know,
In this kingdom by the sea)
That the wind came out of the cloud, chilling
And killing my Annabel Lee.

But our love it was stronger by far than the love
Of those who were older than we –

Of many far wiser than we –
And neither the angels in Heaven above,
Nor the demons down under the sea,
Can ever dissever my soul from the soul
Of the beautiful Annabel Lee.

For the moon never beams without bringing me dreams
Of the beautiful Annabel Lee;
And the stars never rise but I feel the bright eyes
Of the beautiful Annabel Lee;
And so, all the night-tide, I lie down by the side
Of my darling, my darling, my life and my bride,
In the sepulchre there by the sea –
In her tomb by the side of the sea.

John Donne (1572–1631)

Holy Sonnet 10

Death, be not proud, though some have called thee
Mighty and dreadfull, for, thou art not so,
For those whom thou think'st, thou dost overthrow,
Die not, poor Death, nor yet canst thou kill me.
From rest and sleep, which but thy pictures be,
Much pleasure; then from thee much more must flow,
And soonest our best men with thee do go,
Rest of their bones, and souls delivery.
Thou'art slave to fate, chance, kings, and desperate men,
And dost with poison, war, and sickness dwell,
And poppy'or charms can make us sleep as well
And better than thy stroke; why swell'st thou then?
One short sleep past, we wake eternally,
And death shall be no more; Death, thou shalt die.

Walt Whitman (1819–92)

O Captain! My Captain!

O Captain! my Captain! our fearful trip is done,
The ship has weathered every rack, the prize we sought is won,
The port is near, the bells I hear, the people all exulting,
While follow eyes the steady keel, the vessel grim and daring;
But O heart! heart! heart!
O the bleeding drops of red,
Where on the deck my Captain lies,
Fallen cold and dead.

O Captain! my Captain! rise up and hear the bells;
Rise up – for you the flag is flung – for you the bugle trills,
For you bouquets and ribboned wreaths –
    for you the shores a-crowding,
For you they call, the swaying mass, their eager faces turning;
Here Captain! dear father!
This arm beneath your head!
It is some dream that on the deck
You've fallen cold and dead.

My Captain does not answer, his lips are pale and still,
My father does not feel my arm, he has no pulse nor will.
The ship is anchored safe and sound, its
    voyage closed and done;
From fearful trip the victor ship comes in with object won;
Exult O shores, and ring O bells!
But I, with mournful tread,
Walk the deck my Captain lies,
Fallen cold and dead.

Stevie Smith (1902–71)

Not Waving But Drowning

Nobody heard him, the dead man,
But still he lay moaning:
I was much further out than you thought
And not waving but drowning.

Poor chap, he always loved larking
And now he's dead
It must have been too cold for him his heart gave way,
They said.

Oh, no no no, it was too cold always
(Still the dead one lay moaning)
I was much too far out all my life
And not waving but drowning.

Edward Thomas (1878–1917)

In Memoriam (Easter 1915)

The flowers left thick at nightfall in the wood
    This Eastertide call into mind the men,
    Now far from home, who, with their sweethearts, should
    Have gathered them and will do never again.

'Poets put things better than other people – that is what they are for – and it is a pity not to use them... It is easy, after all, to learn a poem and often hard to forget one.'

George Watson, 'The Virtue of Verse', *Times Higher Education*, 29 July 2010

Thirteen

Bugles calling for them: War

There are countless poems inspired by the horrors and heroism of war. In Victorian times, schoolboys were encouraged to learn the most patriotic verses by heart as a way for them to imbibe the values of the Empire. Now, we are more likely to be taught about the terrors of the trenches using the poetry of World War I, proving that poets can move us with their words in ways that textbooks never could.

Rose Macaulay (1881–1958)

Picnic: July 1917

We lay and ate the sweet hurt-berries
In the bracken of Hurt Wood.
Like a quire of singers singing low
The dark pines stood.

Behind us climbed the Surrey Hills,
Wild, wild in greenery;
At our feet the downs of Sussex broke
To an unseen sea.

And life was bound in a still ring,
Drowsy, and quiet and sweet…
When heavily up the south-east wind
The great guns beat.

We did not wince, we did not weep,
We did not curse or pray;
We drowsily heard, and someone said,
'They sound clear today'.

We did not shake with pity and pain,
Or sicken and blanch white.
We said, 'If the wind's from over there
There'll be rain tonight'.

Once pity we knew, and rage we knew,
And pain we knew, too well,
As we stared and peered dizzily
Through the gates of hell.

But now hell's gates are an old tale;
Remote the anguish seems;

The guns are muffled and far away.
Dreams within dreams.

And far and far are Flanders mud,
And the pain of Picardy;
And the blood that runs there runs beyond
The wide waste sea.

We are shut about by guarding walls;
(We have built them lest we run
Mad from dreaming of naked fear
And of black things done).

We are ringed all round by guarding walls,
So high, they shut the view.
Not all the guns that shatter the world
Can quite break through.

Oh guns of France, oh guns of France,
Be still, you crash in vain...
Heavily up the south wind throb
Dull dreams of pain...

Be still, be still, south wind, lest your
Blowing should bring the rain...
We'll lie very quiet on Hurt Hill,
And sleep once again.

Oh we'll lie quite still, not listen nor look,
While the earth's bounds reel and shake,
Lest, battered too long, our walls and we
Should break.......should break..........

Siegfried Sassoon (1886–1967)

The General

'Good-morning; good-morning!' the General said
When we met him last week on our way to the line.
Now the soldiers he smiled at are most of 'em dead,
And we're cursing his staff for incompetent swine.
'He's a cheery old card,' grunted Harry to Jack
As they slogged up to Arras with rifle and pack.

But he did for them both by his plan of attack.

Wilfred Owen (1893–1918)

Dulce et Decorum Est

This is a much-remembered poem, with its savage and searing imagery.

Bent double, like old beggars under sacks,
Knock-kneed, coughing like hags, we cursed through sludge,
Till on the haunting flares we turned our backs
And towards our distant rest began to trudge.
Men marched asleep. Many had lost their boots
But limped on, blood-shod. All went lame; all blind;
Drunk with fatigue; deaf even to the hoots
Of tired, outstripped Five-Nines that dropped behind.

Gas! GAS! Quick, boys!– An ecstasy of fumbling,
Fitting the clumsy helmets just in time;
But someone still was yelling out and stumbling,
And flound'ring like a man in fire or lime…
Dim, through the misty panes and thick green light,

As under a green sea, I saw him drowning.

In all my dreams, before my helpless sight,
He plunges at me, guttering, choking, drowning.

If in smothering dreams you too could pace
Behind the wagon that we flung him in,
And watch the white eyes writhing in his face,
His hanging face, like a devil's sick of sin;
If you could hear, at every jolt, the blood
Come gargling from the froth-corrupted lungs,
Obscene as cancer, bitter as the cud
Of vile, incurable sores on innocent tongues,–
My friend, you would not tell with such high zest
To children ardent for some desperate glory,
The old Lie: Dulce et decorum est
Pro patria mori.

Wilfred Owen (1893–1918)

Anthem for Doomed Youth

What passing-bells for these who die as cattle?
   —Only the monstrous anger of the guns.
   Only the stuttering rifles' rapid rattle
Can patter out their hasty orisons.
No mockeries now for them; no prayers nor bells;
   Nor any voice of mourning save the choirs, —
The shrill, demented choirs of wailing shells;
And bugles calling for them from sad shires.

What candles may be held to speed them all?
   Not in the hands of boys, but in their eyes
Shall shine the holy glimmers of goodbyes.

The pallor of girls' brows shall be their pall;
Their flowers the tenderness of patient minds,
And each slow dusk a drawing-down of blinds.

John McCrae (1872–1918)

In Flanders Fields

In Flanders fields the poppies blow
Between the crosses, row on row,
That mark our place; and in the sky
The larks, still bravely singing, fly
Scarce heard amid the guns below.

We are the Dead. Short days ago
We lived, felt dawn, saw sunset glow,
Loved and were loved, and now we lie
In Flanders fields.

Take up our quarrel with the foe:
To you from failing hands we throw
The torch; be yours to hold it high.
If ye break faith with us who die
We shall not sleep, though poppies grow
In Flanders fields.

Fourteen

Bloody, but unbowed: Courage

These poems serve to remind us that others have struggled and overcome before us. Containing words to have at your beck and call when you are most in need of fortitude, the following collection will help you muster the courage you need to face life's many challenges head on.

Arthur Hugh Clough (1819–61)

Say Not the Struggle Nought Availeth

Say not the struggle nought availeth,
    The labour and the wounds are vain,
The enemy faints not, nor faileth,
    And as things have been, things remain.

If hopes were dupes, fears may be liars;
    It may be, in yon smoke concealed,
Your comrades chase e'en now the fliers,
    And, but for you, possess the field.

For while the tired waves, vainly breaking,
    Seem here no painful inch to gain,
Far back through creeks and inlets making
    Came silent, flooding in, the main.

And not by eastern windows only,
    When daylight comes, comes in the light,
In front the sun climbs slow, how slowly,
    But westward, look, the land is bright.

Felicia Dorothea Hemans (1793–1835)

Casabianca

The boy stood on the burning deck
Whence all but he had fled;
The flame that lit the battle's wreck
Shone round him o'er the dead.

Yet beautiful and bright he stood,
As born to rule the storm –

A creature of heroic blood,
A proud, though child-like form.

The flames rolled on – he would not go
Without his father's word;
That father, faint in death below,
His voice no longer heard.

He called aloud: – 'Say, Father, say,
If yet my task is done?'
He knew not that the chieftain lay
Unconscious of his son.

'Speak, Father!' once again he cried,
'If I may yet be gone!'
And but the booming shots replied,
And fast the flames rolled on.

Upon his brow he felt their breath,
And in his waving hair,
And looked from that lone post of death
In still yet brave despair;

And shouted but once more aloud,
'My Father! must I stay?'
While o'er him fast, through sail and shroud,
The wreathing fires made way.

They wrapt the ship in splendour wild,
They caught the flag on high,
And streamed above the gallant child,
Like banners in the sky.

There came a burst of thunder sound –
The boy – oh! where was he?
Ask of the winds that far around

With fragments strew'd the sea! –

With mast, and helm, and pennon fair,
That well had borne their part,
But the noblest thing that perished there
Was that young faithful heart!

W.E. Henley (1849–1903)

Invictus

*This is a poem that everyone should know, so that you can draw
upon it in life's darkest moments.*

Out of the night that covers me,
Black as the Pit from pole to pole,
I thank whatever gods may be
For my unconquerable soul.

In the fell clutch of circumstance
I have not winced nor cried aloud.
Under the bludgeonings of chance
My head is bloody, but unbowed.

Beyond this place of wrath and tears
Looms but the Horror of the shade,
And yet the menace of the years
Finds, and shall find, me unafraid.

It matters not how strait the gate,
How charged with punishments the scroll,
I am the master of my fate;
I am the captain of my soul.

Rudyard Kipling (1865–1936)

If—

If you can keep your head when all about you
Are losing theirs and blaming it on you,
If you can trust yourself when all men doubt you,
But make allowance for their doubting too;
If you can wait and not be tired by waiting,
Or being lied about, don't deal in lies,
Or being hated, don't give way to hating,
And yet don't look too good, nor talk too wise:

If you can dream – and not make dreams your master;
If you can think – and not make thoughts your aim;
If you can meet with Triumph and Disaster
And treat those two impostors just the same;
If you can bear to hear the truth you've spoken
Twisted by knaves to make a trap for fools,
Or watch the things you gave your life to, broken,
And stoop and build 'em up with worn-out tools:

If you can make one heap of all your winnings
And risk it on one turn of pitch-and-toss,
And lose, and start again at your beginnings
And never breathe a word about your loss;
If you can force your heart and nerve and sinew
To serve your turn long after they are gone,
And so hold on when there is nothing in you
Except the Will which says to them: 'Hold on!'

If you can talk with crowds and keep your virtue,
'Or walk with Kings – nor lose the common touch,
If neither foes nor loving friends can hurt you,

If all men count with you, but none too much;
If you can fill the unforgiving minute
With sixty seconds' worth of distance run,
Yours is the Earth and everything that's in it,
And – which is more – you'll be a Man, my son!

Henry Wadsworth Longfellow (1807–82)

The Building of the Ship [extract]

Sail forth into the sea of life,
O gentle, loving, trusting wife,
And safe from all adversity
Upon the bosom of that sea
Thy comings and thy goings be!
For gentleness and love and trust
Prevail o'er angry wave and gust;
And in the wreck of noble lives
Something immortal still survives!

Thou, too, sail on, O Ship of State!
Sail on, O Union, strong and great!
Humanity with all its fears,
With all the hopes of future years,
Is hanging breathless on thy fate!
We know what Master laid thy keel,
What Workmen wrought thy ribs of steel,
Who made each mast, and sail, and rope,
What anvils rang, what hammers beat,
In what a forge and what a heat
Were shaped the anchors of thy hope!
Fear not each sudden sound and shock,
'T is of the wave and not the rock;

'T is but the flapping of the sail,
And not a rent made by the gale!
In spite of rock and tempest's roar,
In spite of false lights on the shore,
Sail on, nor fear to breast the sea
Our hearts, our hopes, are all with thee,
Our hearts, our hopes, our prayers, our tears,
Our faith triumphant o'er our fears,
Are all with thee, – are all with thee!

Alfred, Lord Tennyson (1809–92)

The Charge of the Light Brigade

This rousing poem includes lines that one – when faced with inexplicable instructions in the workplace or a capricious toddler – might have cause to mutter, albeit with the following slight alteration: 'Ours not to reason why, / Ours but to do and die'.

Half a league, half a league,
   Half a league onward,
All in the valley of Death
   Rode the six hundred.
'Forward, the Light Brigade!
Charge for the guns!' he said:
Into the valley of Death
   Rode the six hundred.

'Forward, the Light Brigade!'
Was there a man dismay'd?
Not tho' the soldier knew
   Some one had blunder'd:
Theirs not to make reply,

Theirs not to reason why,
Theirs but to do and die:
Into the valley of Death
   Rode the six hundred.

Cannon to right of them,
Cannon to left of them,
Cannon in front of them
   Volley'd and thunder'd;
Storm'd at with shot and shell,
Boldly they rode and well,
Into the jaws of Death,
Into the mouth of Hell
   Rode the six hundred.

Flash'd all their sabres bare,
Flash'd as they turn'd in air
Sabring the gunners there,
Charging an army, while
   All the world wonder'd:
Plunged in the battery-smoke
Right thro' the line they broke;
Cossack and Russian
Reel'd from the sabre-stroke
   Shatter'd and sunder'd.
Then they rode back, but not
   Not the six hundred.

Cannon to right of them,
Cannon to left of them,
Cannon behind them
   Volley'd and thunder'd;
Storm'd at with shot and shell,
While horse and hero fell,

They that had fought so well
Came thro' the jaws of Death:
Back from the mouth of Hell,
All that was left of them,
    Left of six hundred.

When can their glory fade?
O the wild charge they made!
    All the world wonder'd.
Honour the charge they made,
Honour the Light Brigade,
    Noble six hundred!

W.H. Auden (1907–73)

Underneath an Abject Willow

Underneath an abject willow,
    Lover, sulk no more:
Act from thought should quickly follow.
    What is thinking for?
Your unique and moping station
    Proves you cold;
    Stand up and fold
Your map of desolation.

Bells that toll across the meadows
    From the sombre spire
Toll for these unloving shadows
    Love does not require.
All that lives may love; why longer
    Bow to loss
    With arms across?

Strike and you shall conquer.

Geese in flocks above you flying,
    Their direction know,
Icy brooks beneath you flowing,
    To their ocean go.
Dark and dull is your distraction:
    Walk then, come,
    No longer numb
Into your satisfaction.

Dylan Thomas (1914–53)

Do Not Go Gentle Into That Good Night

Do not go gentle into that good night,
Old age should burn and rave at close of day;
Rage, rage against the dying of the light.

Though wise men at their end know dark is right,
Because their words had forked no lightning they
Do not go gentle into that good night.

Good men, the last wave by, crying how bright
Their frail deeds might have danced in a green bay,
Rage, rage against the dying of the light.

Wild men who caught and sang the sun in flight,
And learn, too late, they grieved it on its way,
Do not go gentle into that good night.

Grave men, near death, who see with blinding sight
Blind eyes could blaze like meteors and be gay,
Rage, rage against the dying of the light.

And you, my father, there on the sad height,
Curse, bless, me now with your fierce tears, I pray.
Do not go gentle into that good night.
Rage, rage against the dying of the light.

Dorothy Parker (1893–1967)

Résumé

Parker's poem is a little less resoundingly heroic than the others in this chapter, but its message – that you might as well put up with life's slings and arrows – is delivered with her usual quotable style.

Razors pain you;
Rivers are damp;
Acids stain you;
And drugs cause cramp.
Guns aren't lawful;
Nooses give;
Gas smells awful;
You might as well live.

'I have never started a poem yet whose end I knew.
Writing a poem is discovering.'

Robert Frost

Fifteen

Navigating the wicked world: Advice

Some of the finest poems contain a message or motto by which to live. Each identifies something essential for a happy life, from laughter and champagne to being unapologetically and contentedly ordinary. Poets' biographies often suggest they are not faultless mentors for life lessons, but there are wise words here that anyone would do well to memorize.

Ella Wheeler Wilcox (1850–1919)

Solitude

Laugh, and the world laughs with you,
Weep, and you weep alone,
For the sad old earth must borrow its mirth,
But has trouble enough of its own.
Sing, and the hills will answer;
Sigh, it is lost on the air,
The echoes bound to a joyful sound,
But shrink from voicing care.

Rejoice, and men will seek you;
Grieve, and they turn and go.
They want full measure of all your pleasure,
But they do not need your woe.
Be glad, and your friends are many,
Be sad, and you lose them all;
There are none to decline your nectared wine,
But alone you must drink life's gall.

Feast, and your halls are crowded,
Fast, and the world goes by.
Succeed and give – and it helps you live,
But no man can help you die;
There is room in the halls of pleasure
For a large and lordly train,
But one by one we must all file on
Through the narrow aisles of pain.

John Betjeman (1906–84)

How To Get On in Society

Phone for the fish knives, Norman
As cook is a little unnerved;
You kiddies have crumpled the serviettes
And I must have things daintily served.

Are the requisites all in the toilet?
The frills round the cutlets can wait
Till the girl has replenished the cruets
And switched on the logs in the grate.

It's ever so close in the lounge dear,
But the vestibule's comfy for tea
And Howard is riding on horseback
So do come and take some with me.

Now here is a fork for your pastries
And do use the couch for your feet;
I know that I wanted to ask you –
Is trifle sufficient for sweet?

Milk and then just as it comes dear?
I'm afraid the preserve's full of stones;
Beg pardon, I'm soiling the doileys
With afternoon tea-cakes and scones.

Dorothy Parker (1893–1967)

Inventory

Four be the things I am wiser to know:
Idleness, sorrow, a friend, and a foe.

Four be the things I'd been better without:
Love, curiosity, freckles, and doubt.

Three be the things I shall never attain:
Envy, content, and sufficient champagne.

Three be the things I shall have till I die:
Laughter and hope and a sock in the eye.

Philip Larkin (1922–85)

Born Yesterday

Tightly-folded bud,
I have wished you something
None of the others would:
Not the usual stuff
About being beautiful,
Or running off a spring
Of innocence and love —
They will all wish you that,
And should it prove possible,
Well, you're a lucky girl.

But if it shouldn't, then
May you be ordinary;
Have, like other women,
An average of talents:

Not ugly, not good-looking,
Nothing uncustomary
To pull you off your balance,
That, unworkable itself,
Stops all the rest from working.
In fact, may you be dull —
If that is what a skilled,
Vigilant, flexible,
Unemphasised, enthralled
Catching of happiness is called.

Sir Henry Wotton (1568–1639)

The Character of a Happy Life

How *happy* is he born and taught,
That serveth not another's *will*?
Whose *armour* is his *honest thought*,
And simple *truth* his umost *skill*?

Whose *passions* not his *masters* are,
Whose *soul* is still prepar'd for *death*;
Unti'd unto the World by care
Of *publick fame*, or *private breath*.

Who *envies* none whom *chance* doth *raise*,
Or *vice* hath ever understood;
How deepest wounds are giv'n by *praise*,
Nor rules of *State*, but rules of *good*.

Who hath his *life* from *rumours freed*,
Whose *conscience* is his strong *retreat*:
Whose *state* can neither *flatterers feed*,
Nor *ruine* make Oppressors great.

Who *God* doth late and early pray,
More of his *grace* than *gifts* to lend:
And entertains the harmless day
With a *Religious Book*, or Friend.

This man is freed from servile bands,
Of hope to rise, or *fear* to fall:
Lord of himself, though not of *Lands*,
And having *nothing*, yet hath *all*.

Patrick Cary (*c.* 1624–57)

For God's Sake Marcke That Fly

For God's sake marcke that *Fly*:
See what a poore, weake, little Thing itt is.
When Thou hast marck'd, and scorn'd itt; know that This,
This little, poore, weake *Fly*
Has killed a *Pope*; can make an *Emp'rour* dye.

Behold yon *Sparcke of Fire*:
How little hott! How neare to nothing 'tis!
When thou has donne despising, know that this,
This contemn'd *Sparcke of Fire*
Has burn't whole Townes; can burne a World entire.

That crawling *Worme* there see:
Ponder how ugly, filthy, vild Itt is.
When Thou hast seene and loath'd itt, know that This
This base *Worme* Thou doest see,
Has quite devour'd thy Parents; shall eate Thee.

Honour, the *World*, and *Man*,
What Trifles are they! Since most true itt is

That this poore *Fly*, this little *Sparckle*, this
Soe much abhorr'd *Worme*, can
Honour destroy; burne *Worlds*; devoure up *Man*.

Isaac Watts (1674–1748)

The Sluggard

Modern-day audiences tend to be more familiar with Lewis Carroll's delicious parodies than Watts's original improving verses. This rhyme is especially likely to strike a chord with the parents of teenagers.

'Tis the Voice of the Sluggard; I heard him complain,
'You have wak'd me too soon, I must slumber again.'
As the Door on its Hinges, so he on his Bed,
Turns his Sides and his Shoulders and his heavy Head.

'A little more Sleep, and a little more Slumber;'
Thus he wastes half his Days and his Hours without Number;
And when he gets up, he sits folding his Hands,
Or walks about sauntring, or trifling he stands.

I pass'd by his Garden, and saw the wild Brier,
The Thorn and the Thistle grow broader and higher;
The Clothes that hang on him are turning to Rags;
And his Money still wastes, till he starves or he begs.

I made him a Visit, still hoping to find
He had took better Care for improving his Mind:
He told me his Dreams, talk'd of Eating and Drinking;
But he scarce reads his Bible, and never loves Thinking.

Said I then to my Heart, 'Here's a Lesson for me;'
That Man's but a Picture of what I might be:
But thanks to my Friends for their Care in my Breeding,
Who taught me betimes to love Working and Reading.

Mary Howitt (1799–1888)

The Spider and the Fly

'Will you walk into my parlour?' said the Spider to the Fly,
''Tis the prettiest little parlour that ever you did spy;
The way into my parlour is up a winding stair,
And I've a many curious things to shew when you are there.'
'Oh no, no,' said the little Fly, 'to ask me is in vain,
For who goes up your winding stair can ne'er come down again.'

'I'm sure you must be weary, dear, with soaring up so high;
Will you rest upon my little bed?' said the Spider to the Fly.
'There are pretty curtains drawn around; the sheets are fine and
    thin,
And if you like to rest awhile, I'll snugly tuck you in!'
'Oh no, no,' said the little Fly, 'for I've often heard it said,
They never, never wake again, who sleep upon your bed!'

Said the cunning Spider to the Fly, 'Dear friend what can I do,
To prove the warm affection I've always felt for you?
I have within my pantry, good store of all that's nice;
I'm sure you're very welcome – will you please to take a slice?'
'Oh no, no,' said the little Fly, 'kind Sir, that cannot be,
I've heard what's in your pantry, and I do not wish to see!'

'Sweet creature!' said the Spider, 'you're witty and you're wise,
How handsome are your gauzy wings, how brilliant are your
    eyes!

I've a little looking-glass upon my parlour shelf,
If you'll step in one moment, dear, you shall behold yourself.'
'I thank you, gentle sir,' she said, 'for what you're pleased to say,
And bidding you good morning now, I'll call another day.'

The Spider turned him round about, and went into his den,
For well he knew the silly Fly would soon come back again:
So he wove a subtle web, in a little corner sly,
And set his table ready, to dine upon the Fly.
Then he came out to his door again, and merrily did sing,
'Come hither, hither, pretty Fly, with the pearl and silver wing;
Your robes are green and purple – there's a crest upon your head;
Your eyes are like the diamond bright, but mine are dull as lead!'

Alas, alas! How very soon this silly little Fly,
Hearing his wily, flattering words, came slowly flitting by;
With buzzing wings she hung aloft, then near and nearer drew,
Thinking only of her brilliant eyes, and green and purple hue –
Thinking only of her crested head – poor foolish thing! At last,
Up jumped the cunning Spider, and fiercely held her fast.
He dragged her up his winding stair, into his dismal den,
Within his little parlour – but she ne'er came out again!

And now dear little children, who may this story read,
To idle, silly flattering words, I pray you ne'er give heed:
Unto an evil counsellor, close heart and ear and eye,
And take a lesson from this tale, of the Spider and the Fly.

Hilaire Belloc (1870–1953)

Henry King (Who chewed bits of String, and was early cut off in Dreadful Agonies)

Belloc's 1907 Cautionary Tales *includes poems replete with all sorts of sensible advice, and their rhyme and rhythm make them easy to learn. It's hard to know how prevalent the evil of string chewing is among today's youth, but arm yourself with this verse just in case you have to deliver such a lecture.*

The Chief Defect of Henry King
Was chewing little bits of String.
At last he swallowed some which tied
Itself in ugly Knots inside.

Physicians of the Utmost Fame
Were called at once; but when they came
They answered, as they took their Fees,
'There is no Cure for this Disease.
Henry will very soon be dead.'
His parents stood about his Bed
Lamenting his Untimely Death,
When Henry, with his Latest Breath,
Cried–'Oh, my Friends, be warned by me,
That Breakfast, Dinner, Lunch and Tea
Are all the Human Frame requires...'
With that, the Wretched Child expires.

Dorothy Parker (1893–1967)

Observation

If I don't drive around the park,
I'm pretty sure to make my mark.
If I'm in bed each night by ten,
I may get back my looks again.
If I abstain from fun and such,
I'll probably amount to much;
But I shall stay the way I am,
Because I do not give a damn.

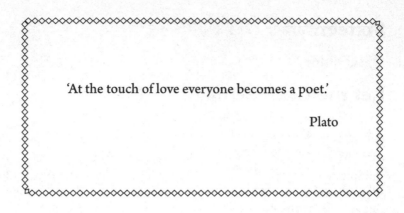

'At the touch of love everyone becomes a poet.'

Plato

Sixteen

Let the Lord be thankit: Faith

For many generations poetry was absorbed through familiarity with the services of the church. Today, in more secular times, children tend not to imbibe the verses that were so much a part of their ancestors' consciousness but, whatever your religious affinity, it seems a shame not to embrace the sonorous language of the Bible. Here, then, are poems with a divine flavour – some grandiose and others less so – which lend themselves beautifully to being learned by heart.

Robert Burns (1759–96)

Kirkcudbright Grace

Some have meat and cannot eat,
    Some cannot eat that want it:
But we have meat and we can eat,
    Sae let the Lord be thankit.

John Donne (1572–1631)

Holy Sonnet 14

Batter my heart, three-personed God; for You
As yet but knock; breathe, shine, and seek to mend;
That I may rise and stand, o'erthrow me,' and bend
Your force to break, blow, burn, and make me new.
I, like an usurped town, to'another due,
Labor to'admit You, but O, to no end;
Reason, Your viceroy in me, me should defend,
But is captived, and proves weak or untrue.
Yet dearly'I love you,' and would be loved fain,
But am betrothed unto your enemy.
Divorce me, 'untie or break that knot again;
Take me to you, imprison me, for I,
Except you'enthrall me, never shall be free,
Nor ever chaste, except you ravish me.

J. C. Squire (1884–1958)

The Dilemma

God heard the embattled nations sing and shout
'Gott strafe England!' and 'God save the King!'
God this, God that, and God the other thing –
'Good God!' said God 'I've got my work cut out.'

Emily Dickinson (1830–86)

202/185

'Faith' is a fine invention
When Gentlemen can see—
But Microscopes are prudent
In an Emergency.

William Cowper (1731–1800)

Light Shining out of Darkness

Sense and Sensibility's *Marianne Dashwood fiercely condemns
Edward Ferrars for his impassive reading of Cowper – 'It would
have broken my heart, had I loved him, to hear him read with
so little sensibility.' – so do be sure to infuse his lines with the
requisite passion.*

God moves in a mysterious way,
His wonders to perform,
He plants his footsteps in the Sea,
And rides upon the Storm.

Deep in unfathomable Mines
Of never failing Skill,
He treasures up his bright designs,
And works his Sovereign Will.

Ye fearfull Saints fresh courage take,
The clouds ye so much dread,
Are big with Mercy, and shall break
In blessings on your head.

Judge not the Lord by feeble sense,
But trust him for his Grace,
Behind a frowning Providence
He hides a Smiling face.

His purposes will ripen fast,
Unfolding every hour,
The Bud may have a bitter taste,
But *wait, to smell the flower.*

Blind unbelief is sure to err,
And scan his work in vain,
God is his own Interpreter,
And he will make it plain.

John Milton (1608–74)

On His Blindness

When I consider how my light is spent
    Ere half my days in this dark world and wide,
    And that one talent which is death to hide
    Lodg'd with me useless, though my soul more bent
    To serve therewith my Maker, and present
    My true account, lest he returning chide,
    'Doth God exact day-labour, light denied?'
    I fondly ask. But Patience, to prevent
    That murmur, soon replies: 'God doth not need
    Either man's work or his own gifts: who best
    Bear his mild yoke, they serve him best. His state
    Is kingly; thousands at his bidding speed
    And post o'er land and ocean without rest:
    They also serve who only stand and wait.'

'Poetry is not only dream and vision; it is the skeleton architecture of our lives. It lays the foundations for a future of change, a bridge across our fears of what has never been before.'

Audre Lorde

Seventeen

The music makers: Poets and Poetry

The following collection contains poems that have been written about poets and poetry. Some celebrate the magic woven by the bards, and some are more down-to-earth in their assessment – but all are worth memorizing for future reference.

Howard Nemerov (1920–99)

Strange Metamorphosis of Poets

From epigram to epic is the course
For riders of the American winged horse.
They change both size and sex over the years,
The voice grows deeper and the beard appears;
Running for greatness they sweat away their salt,
They start out Emily and wind up Walt.

Arthur O'Shaughnessy (1844–81)

Ode 'We are the music makers'

We are the music-makers,
And we are the dreamers of dreams,
Wandering by lone sea-breakers,
And sitting by desolate streams;
World-losers and world-forsakers,
On whom the pale moon gleams:
Yet we are the movers and shakers
Of the world for ever, it seems.

With wonderful deathless ditties
We build up the world's great cities,
And out of a fabulous story
We fashion an empire's glory:
One man with a dream, at pleasure,
Shall go forth and conquer a crown;
And three with a new song's measure
Can trample an empire down.

We, in the ages lying
In the buried past of the earth,
Built Nineveh with our sighing,
And Babel itself with our mirth;
And o'erthrew them with prophesying
To the old of the new world's worth;
For each age is a dream that is dying,
Or one that is coming to birth.

John Keats (1795–1821)

On First Looking Into Chapman's Homer

Much have I travell'd in the realms of gold,
And many goodly states and kingdoms seen;
Round many western islands have I been
Which bards in fealty to Apollo hold.
Oft of one wide expanse had I been told
That deep-brow'd Homer ruled as his demesne;
Yet did I never breathe its pure serene
Till I heard Chapman speak out loud and bold:
Then felt I like some watcher of the skies
When a new planet swims into his ken;
Or like stout Cortez when with eagle eyes
He star'd at the Pacific—and all his men
Look'd at each other with a wild surmise—
Silent, upon a peak in Darien.

Edgell Rickword (1898–1982)

Trench Poets

Here is a moving testament to poetry as something to cling to in terrible times.

I knew a man, he was my chum,
But he grew blacker every day,
And would not brush the flies away,
Nor blanch however fierce the hum
Of passing shells; I used to read,
To rouse him, random things from Donne;

Like 'Get with child a mandrake-root,'
But you can tell he was far gone,
For he lay gaping, mackerel-eyed,
And stiff, and senseless as a post
Even when that old poet cried
'I long to talk with some old lover's ghost.'

I tried the Elegies one day,
But he, because he heard me say
'What needst thou have more covering than a man?'
Grinned nastily, and so I knew
The worms had got his brains at last.
There was one thing that I might do
To starve the worms; I racked my head
For healthy things and quoted '*Maud.*'
His grin got worse and I could see
He sneered at passion's purity.
He stank so badly, though we were great chums
I had to leave him; then rats ate his thumbs.

Walt Whitman (1819–92)

Song of Myself [extract]

I celebrate myself, and sing myself,
And what I assume you shall assume,
For every atom belonging to me as good belongs to you.

I loafe and invite my soul,
I lean and loafe at my ease observing a spear of summer grass.

My tongue, every atom of my blood, form'd from this soil, this air,
Born here of parents born here from parents the same, and their
    parents the same,
I, now thirty-seven years old in perfect health begin,
Hoping to cease not till death.

Creeds and schools in abeyance,
Retiring back a while sufficed at what they are, but never forgotten,
I harbor for good or bad, I permit to speak at every hazard,
Nature without check with original energy.

Dorothy Parker (1893–1967)

Oscar Wilde

If, with the literate, I am
    Impelled to try an epigram,
    I never seek to take the credit;
    We all assume that Oscar said it.

'Prose = words in their best order; poetry = the best words in the best order.'

Samuel Taylor Coleridge

Eighteen

Last night's loud long how-do-you-do: Making Merry

Here are words for carousing and carolling – and, in Lowry's case, enduring the aftermath – rather than reflecting on. Drinking songs have always formed part of most cultures, from taverns to the football terraces, and a steady rhythm and clear rhyme scheme enable them to be committed easily to memory by a great number of celebrants. Herewith you will also find poems about Christmas, some of which will be familiar from childhood.

Abraham Cowley (1618–67)

Drinking

The thirsty *Earth* soaks up the *Rain*,
And drinks, and gapes for drink again.
The *Plants* suck in the *Earth*, and are
With constant drinking fresh and fair.
The *Sea* itself, which one would think
Should have but little need of *Drink*,
Drinks ten thousand *Rivers* up,
So fill'd that they o'erflow the *Cup*.
The busie *Sun* (and one would guess
By's drunken fiery face no less)
Drinks up the *Sea*, and when h'as done,
The *Moon* and *Stars* drink up the *Sun*.
       They drink and dance by their own light,
They drink and revel all the night.
Nothing in *Nature's Sober* found,
But an eternal *Health* goes round.
Fill up the *Bowl* then, fill it high,
Fill all the *Glasses* there, for why
Should every creature drink but *I*,
Why, *Man* of *Morals*, tell me why?

Louis MacNeice (1907–63)

Bagpipe Music

It's no go the merrygoround, it's no go the rickshaw,
All we want is a limousine and a ticket for the peepshow.
Their knickers are made of crêpe-de-chine, their shoes are made
   of python,

Their halls are lined with tiger rugs and their walls with heads of
    bison.

John MacDonald found a corpse, put it under the sofa,
Waited till it came to life and hit it with a poker,
Sold its eyes for souvenirs, sold its blood for whisky,
Kept its bones for dumbbells to use when he was fifty.

It's no go the Yogi-Man, it's no go Blavatsky,
All we want is a bank balance and a bit of skirt in a taxi.

Annie MacDougall went to milk, caught her foot in the heather,
Woke to hear a dance record playing of Old Vienna.
It's no go your maidenheads, it's no go your culture,
All we want is a Dunlop tyre and the devil mend the puncture.

The Laird o' Phelps spent Hogmanay declaring he was sober,
Counted his feet to prove the fact and found he had one foot
    over.
Mrs. Carmichael had her fifth, looked at the job with repulsion,
Said to the midwife 'Take it away; I'm through with
    over-production'.

It's no go the gossip column, it's no go the ceilidh,
All we want is a mother's help and a sugar-stick for the baby.

Willie Murray cut his thumb, couldn't count the damage,
Took the hide of an Ayrshire cow and used it for a bandage.
His brother caught three hundred cran when the seas were lavish,
Threw the bleeders back in the sea and went upon the parish.

It's no go the Herring Board, it's no go the Bible,
All we want is a packet of fags when our hands are idle.

It's no go the picture palace, it's no go the stadium,
It's no go the country cot with a pot of pink geraniums,

It's no go the Government grants, it's no go the elections,
Sit on your arse for fifty years and hang your hat on a pension.

It's no go my honey love, it's no go my poppet;
Work your hands from day to day, the winds will blow the profit.
The glass is falling hour by hour, the glass will fall for ever,
But if you break the bloody glass you won't hold up the weather.

Malcolm Lowry (1909–57)

Eye-Opener

How like a man, is Man, who rises late
And gazes on his unwashed dinner plate
And gazes on the bottles, empty too,
All gulphed in last night's loud long how-do-you-do,
—Although one glass yet holds a gruesome bate—
How like to Man is this man and his fate—
Still drunk and stumbling through the rusty trees
To breakfast on stale rum sardines and peas.

John Betjeman (1906–84)

Christmas

The bells of waiting Advent ring,
The Tortoise stove is lit again
And lamp-oil light across the night
Has caught the streaks of winter rain
In many a stained-glass window sheen
From Crimson Lake to Hookers Green.

The holly in the windy hedge

And round the Manor House the yew
Will soon be stripped to deck the ledge,
The altar, font and arch and pew,
So that the villagers can say
'The church looks nice' on Christmas Day.

Provincial Public Houses blaze,
Corporation tramcars clang,
On lighted tenements I gaze,
Where paper decorations hang,
And bunting in the red Town Hall
Says 'Merry Christmas to you all'.

And London shops on Christmas Eve
Are strung with silver bells and flowers
As hurrying clerks the City leave
To pigeon-haunted classic towers,
And marbled clouds go scudding by
The many-steepled London sky.

And girls in slacks remember Dad,
And oafish louts remember Mum,
And sleepless children's hearts are glad.
And Christmas-morning bells say 'Come!'
Even to shining ones who dwell
Safe in the Dorchester Hotel.

And is it true,
This most tremendous tale of all,
Seen in a stained-glass window's hue,
A Baby in an ox's stall?
The Maker of the stars and sea
Become a Child on earth for me?

And is it true? For if it is,

No loving fingers tying strings
Around those tissued fripperies,
The sweet and silly Christmas things,
Bath salts and inexpensive scent
And hideous tie so kindly meant,

No love that in a family dwells,
No carolling in frosty air,
Nor all the steeple-shaking bells
Can with this single Truth compare –
That God was man in Palestine
And lives today in Bread and Wine.

Clement C. Moore (1799–1863)

Account of a Visit from St. Nicholas

This is a poem much beloved of children and full of nostalgic pleasure for grown-ups. Should you choose to learn it, you will never be stumped by a quiz question about the names of Santa's reindeer.

'Twas the night before Christmas, when all through the house
Not a creature was stirring, not even a mouse;
The stockings were hung by the chimney with care,
In hopes that St Nicholas soon would be there;
The children were nestled all snug in their beds,
While visions of sugar plums danced in their heads,
And mamma in her 'kerchief, and I in my cap,
Had just settled our brains for a long winter's nap,
When out on the lawn there arose such a clatter,
I sprang from the bed to see what was the matter.
Away to the window I flew like a flash,

Tore open the shutters, and threw up the sash.
The moon on the breast of the new fallen snow,
Gave the luster of mid-day to objects below;
When, what to my wondering eyes should appear,
But a miniature sleigh, and eight tiny reindeer,
With a little old driver, so lively and quick,
I knew in a moment it must be St Nick.
More rapid than eagles his coursers they came,
And he whistled, and shouted, and call'd them by name,
'Now! Dasher! now, Dancer! now, Prancer and Vixen!
'On, Comet! on, Cupid! on, Dunder and Blitzem!
'To the top of the porch! To the top of the wall!
'Now dash away! Dash away! Dash away all!'
As dry leaves that before the wild hurricane fly,
When they meet with an obstacle, mount to the sky;
So up to the house top the coursers they flew,
With the sleigh full of toys, and St Nicholas, too.
And then in a twinkling, I heard on the roof
The prancing and pawing of each little hoof.
As I drew in my head, and was turning around,
Down the chimney St Nicholas came with a bound.
He was dressed all in fur, from his head to his foot,
And his clothes were all tarnish'd with ashes and soot;
A bundle of toys he had flung on his back,
And he looked like a peddler just opening his pack.
His eyes – how they twinkled – his dimples how merry!
His cheeks were like roses, his nose like a cherry;
His droll little mouth was drawn up like a bow,
And the beard of his chin was as white as the snow;
The stump of a pipe he held tight in his teeth,
And the smoke it encircled his head like a wreath;
He had a broad face, and a little round belly,

That shook when he laughed, like a bowlful of jelly.
He was chubby and plump, a right jolly old elf,
And I laughed when I saw him, in spite of myself;
A wink of his eye and a twist of his head
Soon gave me to know I had nothing to dread.
He spoke not a word, but went straight to his work,
And filled all the stockings; then turned with a jerk,
And laying his finger aside of his nose,
And giving a nod, up the chimney he rose;
He sprang to his sleigh, to his team gave a whistle,
And away they all flew, like the down of a thistle;
But I heard him exclaim, ere he drove out of sight,
'Happy Christmas to all, and to all a good night!'

Henry Wadsworth Longfellow (1807–82)

Christmas Bells

I heard the bells on Christmas Day
Their old familiar carols play,
      And wild and sweet
      The words repeat
Of peace on earth, good-will to men!

And thought how, as the day had come,
The belfries of all Christendom
      Had rolled along
      The unbroken song
Of peace on earth, good-will to men!

Till, ringing, singing on its way,
The world revolved from night to day,
      A voice, a chime,

A chant sublime
Of peace on earth, good-will to men!

Then from each black accursed mouth
The cannon thundered in the South,
And with the sound
The carols drowned
Of peace on earth, good-will to men!

It was as if an earthquake rent
The hearth-stones of a continent,
And made forlorn
The households born
Of peace on earth, good-will to men!

And in despair I bowed my head;
'There is no peace on earth,' I said;
'For hate is strong,
And mocks the song
Of peace on earth, good-will to men!'

Then pealed the bells more loud and deep:
'God is not dead; nor doth he sleep!
The Wrong shall fail,
The Right prevail,
With peace on earth, good-will to men!'

'Poetry is the language in which man explores his own amazement . . . says heaven and earth in one word . . . speaks of himself and his predicament as though for the first time.'

Christopher Fry

Nineteen

Things of beauty: Miscellaneous

This final section includes poems that would not sit easily in any other chapter, but would be a real pleasure to learn and know.

John Keats (1795–1821)

Endymion [extract]

A thing of beauty is a joy for ever:
Its loveliness increases; it will never
Pass into nothingness; but still will keep
A bower quiet for us, and a sleep
Full of sweet dreams, and health, and quiet breathing.
Therefore, on every morrow, are we wreathing
A flowery band to bind us to the earth,
Spite of despondence, of the inhuman dearth
Of noble natures, of the gloomy days,
Of all the unhealthy and o'er-darkened ways
Made for our searching: yes, in spite of all,
Some shape of beauty moves away the pall
From our dark spirits. Such the sun, the moon,
Trees old and young, sprouting a shady boon
For simple sheep; and such are daffodils
With the green world they live in; and clear rills
That for themselves a cooling covert make
'Gainst the hot season; the mid forest brake,
Rich with a sprinkling of fair musk-rose blooms:
And such too is the grandeur of the dooms
We have imagined for the mighty dead;
All lovely tales that we have heard or read —
An endless fountain of immortal drink,
Pouring unto us from the heaven's brink.

T.S. Eliot (1888–1965)

The Love Song of J. Alfred Prufrock [extract]

Let us go then, you and I,
When the evening is spread out against the sky
Like a patient etherised upon a table;
Let us go, through certain half-deserted streets,
The muttering retreats
Of restless nights in one-night cheap hotels
And sawdust restaurants with oyster-shells:
Streets that follow like a tedious argument
Of insidious intent
To lead you to an overwhelming question …
Oh, do not ask, 'What is it?'
Let us go and make our visit.

In the room the women come and go
Talking of Michelangelo.

The yellow fog that rubs its back upon the window-panes,
The yellow smoke that rubs its muzzle on the window-panes,
Licked its tongue into the corners of the evening,
Lingered upon the pools that stand in drains,
Let fall upon its back the soot that falls from chimneys,
Slipped by the terrace, made a sudden leap,
And seeing that it was a soft October night,
Curled once about the house, and fell asleep.

And indeed there will be time
For the yellow smoke that slides along the street
Rubbing its back upon the window-panes;
There will be time, there will be time
To prepare a face to meet the faces that you meet;

There will be time to murder and create,
And time for all the works and days of hands
That lift and drop a question on your plate;
Time for you and time for me,
And time yet for a hundred indecisions,
And for a hundred visions and revisions,
Before the taking of a toast and tea.

In the room the women come and go
   Talking of Michelangelo.

Robert Frost (1874–1963)

Mending Wall

Something there is that doesn't love a wall,
That sends the frozen-ground-swell under it,
And spills the upper boulders in the sun;
And makes gaps even two can pass abreast.
The work of hunters is another thing:
I have come after them and made repair
Where they have left not one stone on a stone,
But they would have the rabbit out of hiding,
To please the yelping dogs. The gaps I mean,
No one has seen them made or heard them made,
But at spring mending-time we find them there.
I let my neighbor know beyond the hill;
And on a day we meet to walk the line
And set the wall between us once again.
We keep the wall between us as we go.
To each the boulders that have fallen to each.
And some are loaves and some so nearly balls
We have to use a spell to make them balance:

'Stay where you are until our backs are turned!'
We wear our fingers rough with handling them.
Oh, just another kind of outdoor game,
One on a side. It comes to little more:
There where it is we do not need the wall:
He is all pine and I am apple orchard.
My apple trees will never get across
And eat the cones under his pines, I tell him.
He only says, 'Good fences make good neighbours.'
Spring is the mischief in me, and I wonder
If I could put a notion in his head:
'*Why* do they make good neighbours? Isn't it
Where there are cows? But here there are no cows.
Before I built a wall I'd ask to know
What I was walling in or walling out,
And to whom I was like to give offense.
Something there is that doesn't love a wall,
That wants it down.' I could say 'Elves' to him,
But it's not elves exactly, and I'd rather
He said it for himself. I see him there
Bringing a stone grasped firmly by the top
In each hand, like an old-stone savage armed.
He moves in darkness as it seems to me,
Not of woods only and the shade of trees.
He will not go behind his father's saying,
And he likes having thought of it so well
He says again, 'Good fences make good neighbours.'

Edward Lear (1812–88)

How Pleasant to Know Mr Lear

Lear's limericks and nonsense verses are easily committed to memory because of their strong rhythm. This self-deprecating verse is a personal favourite, and includes a runcible hat to match the Owl and Pussy-cat's spoon.

How pleasant to know Mr. Lear!
  Who has written such volumes of stuff!
Some think him ill-tempered and queer,
  But a few think him pleasant enough.

His mind is concrete and fastidious,
  His nose is remarkably big;
His visage is more or less hideous,
  His beard it resembles a wig.

He has ears, and two eyes, and ten fingers,
  Leastways if you reckon two thumbs;
Long ago he was one of the singers,
  But now he is one of the dumbs.

He sits in a beautiful parlor,
  With hundreds of books on the wall;
He drinks a great deal of Marsala,
  But never gets tipsy at all.

He has many friends, laymen and clerical;
  Old Foss is the name of his cat;
His body is perfectly spherical,
  He weareth a runcible hat.

When he walks in waterproof white,
   The children run after him so!
Calling out, 'He's gone out in his night-
   Gown, that crazy old Englishman, oh!'

He weeps by the side of the ocean,
   He weeps on the top of the hill;
He purchases pancakes and lotion,
   And chocolate shrimps from the mill.

He reads but he cannot speak Spanish,
   He cannot abide ginger-beer:
Ere the days of his pilgrimage vanish,
   How pleasant to know Mr. Lear!

Edward Lear (1812–88)

There Was an Old Man With a Beard

There was an Old Man with a beard,
Who said, 'It is just as I feared!—
Two Owls and a Hen, four Larks and a Wren,
Have all built their nests in my beard!'

William Carlos Williams (1883–1963)

The Red Wheelbarrow

so much depends
upon

a red wheel
barrow

glazed with rain
water

beside the white
chickens.

William Wordsworth (1770–1850)

Composed Upon Westminster Bridge, Semptember 3, 1802

Earth has not anything to show more fair:
Dull would he be of soul who could pass by
A sight so touching in its majesty:
This City now doth, like a garment, wear
The beauty of the morning; silent, bare,
Ships, towers, domes, theatres, and temples lie
Open unto the fields, and to the sky;
All bright and glittering in the smokeless air.
Never did sun more beautifully steep
In his first splendour, valley, rock, or hill;
Ne'er saw I, never felt, a calm so deep!
The river glideth at his own sweet will:
Dear God! the very houses seem asleep;
And all that mighty heart is lying still!

Select Bibliography

Abrams, M.H. (ed.), *The Norton Anthology of English Literature, Volume I* (W W Norton, 1993)

Abrams, M.H., et al (eds), *The Norton Anthology of English Literature Volume II* (W W Norton, 1993)

Barber, Laura (ed.), *Penguin's Poems by Heart: Poetry to Remember and Love For Ever* (Penguin, 2009)

Creighton, T.R.N. (ed.), *Poems of Thomas Hardy, A New Selection* (Macmillan, 1974)

Donoghue, Denis, *Yeats* (Fontana, 1971)

Eliot, T.S., *Old Possum's Book of Practical Cats* (Faber, 1939)

Eliot, T.S., *Selected Poems* (Faber, 1954)

Ferguson, Margaret, Salter, Mary Jo and Stallworthy, Jon (eds), *The Norton Anthology of Poetry* (W W Norton, 2005)

Gill, Brendan (ed.), *The Collected Dorothy Parker* (Penguin, 2001)

Gurr, Elizabeth and de Piro, Celia, (eds), *Nineteenth and Twentieth Century Women Poets* (Oxford University Press, 2006)

Hamilton, Ian (ed.), *The Oxford Companion to Twentieth-Century Poetry in English* (Oxford University Press, 1994)

Hayward, John (ed.), *Robert Herrick: Selected Poems* (Penguin, 1961)

Heaney, Seamus (ed.), *William Wordsworth* (Faber, 2001)

Holmes, Richard, *Blake's Songs of Innocence and Experience* (Tate Publishing, 1991)

Hughes, Ted (ed.), *By Heart: 101 Poems to Remember* (Faber, 1997)

McDonald, Trevor, *Favourite Poems* (Michael O'Mara, 1997)

Ricks, Christopher (ed.), *The Oxford Book of English Verse* (Oxford University Press, 1999)

Roe, Dinah (ed.), *The Pre-Raphaelites: From Rossetti to Ruskin* (Penguin, 2010)

Sampson, Ana (ed.), *I Wandered Lonely as a Cloud... and other poems you half-remember from school* (Michael O'Mara, 2009)

Sampson, Ana (ed.), *Tyger Tyger, Burning Bright: Much-Loved Poems You Half Remember* (Michael O'Mara, 2011)

Walter, George (ed.), *The Penguin Book of First World War Poetry* (Penguin, 2006)

Williams, Hugo (ed.), *John Betjeman* (Faber, 2006)

Acknowledgements

The author and publishers are grateful to the following for permission to use material that is in copyright:

Matthew Arnold: 'Dover Beach' by Matthew Arnold reproduced by kind permission of Frederick Whitridge.

W.H. Auden: 'Funeral Blues' and 'Underneath an Abject Willow' copyright © 1936, 1938, 1940 by W. H. Auden, renewed. Reprinted by permission of Curtis Brown, Ltd.

Hilaire Belloc: 'Henry King' from *Cautionary Tales for Children* by Hilaire Belloc reprinted with permission of Peters, Fraser & Dunlop (www.petersfraserdunlop.com) on behalf of the Estate of Hilaire Belloc.

John Betjeman: 'How To Get On in Society,' 'Christmas' and 'Slough' by John Betjeman from *Collected Poems* (John Murray) by John Betjeman, by permission of John Murray (Publishers).

Louise Bogan: 'Juan's Song' from *The Blue Estuaries* by Louise Bogan. Copyright © 1968 by Louise Bogan. Copyright renewed 1996 by Ruth Limmer. Reprinted by permission of Farrar, Straus and Giroux, LLC.

Lord George Gordon Byron: 'When We Two Parted' and 'The Destruction of Sennacherib' by permission of John Murray Publishers.

Samuel Taylor Coleridge: Extracts from 'Kubla Khan, or A Vision in a Dream. A Fragment.' and 'The Rime of the Ancient Mariner' by kind permission of Mrs Priscilla Coleridge Cassam.

Wendy Cope: 'Valentine' from *Serious Concerns*, by Wendy Cope (Faber and Faber, 2002) reprinted by permission of United Agents on behalf of Wendy Cope.

Rose Macaulay: 'Picnic: July 1917' by Rose Macaulay
by permission of The Society of Authors as the Literary
Representative of the Estate of Rose Macaulay.

Louise Macneice: 'Bagpipe Music' by Louise Macneice, from
Selected Poems (Faber and Faber), by permission of David Higham
Associates Ltd.

Walter de la Mare: 'The Listeners' by Walter de la Mare by
permission of The Literary Trustees of Walter de la Mare and The
Society of Authors as their Representative.

John Masefield: 'Sea-Fever' by John Masefield by permission of
The Society of Authors as the Literary Representative of the Estate
of John Masefield.

A.A. Milne: 'Disobedience' from *When We Were Very Young* by
A.A. Milne. Text copyright © The Trustees of Pooh Properties
1924. Published by Egmont UK Ltd. London and used
with permission.

Howard Moss: 'Tourists' by Howard Moss, reproduced with kind
permission of the Estate of Howard Moss.

Howard Nemerov: 'Strange Metamorphosis of Poets' by Howard
Nemerov courtesy the Estate of Howard Nemerov.

Wilfred Owen: 'Dulce et Decorum Est' and 'Anthem for Doomed
Youth' by Wilfred Owen from *Wilfred Owen: The War Poems*, ed.
John Stallworthy (Chatto & Windus, 1994).

Dorothy Parker: 'The Lady's Reward', 'Résumé', 'Inventory',
'Observation' and 'Oscar Wilde' by Dorothy Parker by permission
of Gerald Duckworth & Co Ltd.

Edgell Rickword: 'Trench Poets' by Edgell Rickword from *Collected
Poems*, ed. Charles Hobday (Carcanet Press Limited, 1991).

Index of Poets

Index of Titles, First Lines and Well-Known Lines

Titles of poems are in **bold** type, first lines are in roman type, and familiar or well-known lines are in *italic* type following a headword in ***bold italics***.

When lovely woman stoops to
folly 60
**When Lovely Woman Stoops to
Folly** 60
When the Present has latched its
postern behind my tremulous
stay 122
When we two parted 63
When We Two Parted 63–4
When You Are Old 124
When you are old and grey and full
of sleep 124
Where dost thou careless lie 73
Where the bee sucks, there suck
I 85
Whiting and A Snail, A 98–9
Whose woods these are I think I
know 106
why: Theirs not to reason w. 150
'Will you walk a little faster?' said a
whiting to a snail 98
'Will you walk into my parlour?'
said the Spider to the Fly 162
willow: Underneath an abject w.
151
Windhover, The 95
*wine: And lives today in Bread and
W.* 184
winter: In w. I get up at night 88
*witches: Faster than fairies, faster
than w.* 38
*wolf: The Assyrian came down like
the w. on the fold* 28
*women: In the room the women
come and go* 191, 192
wonders: His w. to perform 169
*woods: The w. are lovely, dark and
deep* 106

*work: 'Good God!' said God 'I've got
my w. cut out.'* 169
*working: Who taught me betimes to
love W. and Reading* 161
*world: A w. of worlds, as pendents in
each ear* 89

Xanadu: In X. did Kubla Khan 14

year: The darkest evening of the y.
106
*years: Hours, days, and y. slide soft
away* 105
young: As I was helplessly y. 117

I Wandered Lonely as a Cloud …
by Ana Sampson

978-1-84317-394-6 in hardback print format
£9.99

978-1-78243-012-4 in paperback print format
£5.99

Tyger Tyger Burning Bright
by Ana Sampson

978-1-84317-594-0 in hardback print format
£9.99